W9-AEZ-003

WINGATE JUNIOR COLLEGE

CAN AMERICA STAY NEUTRAL?

CAN AMERICA STAY NEUTRAL?

BY

ALLEN W. DULLES

AND

HAMILTON FISH ARMSTRONG

HARPER & BROTHERS PUBLISHERS

NEW YORK   LONDON

WINGATE JUNIOR COLLEGE

4427

PREFATORY NOTE

We have received much help from associates and friends in preparing this book, and are duly grateful. We are especially indebted to Mr. Oliver J. Lissitzyn, whose advice has been most useful throughout, and to Mr. William O. Scroggs, who has provided us with material on the American experience during the Napoleonic Wars as well as the trade statistics included in the Appendix. Miss Wilya Gallus has prepared the Chronology, and Mr. Melville Ruggles the Bibliography. The views expressed in these pages, however, engage the responsibility of nobody except ourselves.

A. W. D.
H. F. A.

New York, September 21, 1939

Copyright, 1939, by Harper & Brothers
Printed in the United States of America

CONTENTS

INTRODUCTION

When the present authors wrote "Can We Be Neutral?" late in 1935 the Neutrality Act passed by Congress on August 31 of that year had just started the United States along the road of trying to enforce peace by domestic legislation. Certain sections of that earlier volume appear again here. But momentous events have meanwhile occurred in the world, reënforcing our views in some respects, modifying them in others. Our present task is to bring the story down to date. This involves trying to describe how American neutrality legislation actually operated during the three wars which began in widely separated parts of the world in 1935, 1936 and 1937, and what may be its effect for us in the mighty struggle now joined in Europe.

The present cataclysm has been long in preparation. The international crisis entered an acute stage a year ago, reached a temporary culmination in the Munich settlement of last September, and drifted from bad to worse following the German seizure of the Czech lands of Bohemia and Moravia in March. On September 1, all attempts to dissuade Hitler having failed, his troops attacked Poland; and on September 3 Britain and France declared war on Germany, opening a conflict of unpredictable dimensions and duration. On September 5 President Roosevelt issued two proclamations, one in accordance with the traditional neutrality policy of the United States, the other in the specific sense required by the 1937 Act. On September 21, the day this book went to

1

press, he gave a special session of Congress his recommendations regarding the neutrality policy which the United States should follow in the present crisis. Though the book was already in the hands of the printer, we have found it possible to include the President's message in the Appendix.

We try to accomplish two things in these pages. We try to draw the lessons from past experience as to the practicability and wisdom of attempting to legislate in advance the precise manner in which our Government must always proceed in the dual effort to keep the country at peace and guard its vital interests. And we try to indicate what lessons our actual experience in recent wars carries for Congress and the public in the present war in Europe. The difficulty even today of foreseeing our exactly proper course in the months ahead, and tying the Government to follow it in unvarying detail, must be manifest. For even though the war has already begun, the full list of the protagonists may not yet have been revealed, and their full objectives remain undisclosed and indeed beyond calculation.

CHAPTER I

NEUTRALITY:
POLICY NOT LAW

As the World War drew into perspective, only one clear determination was left in most American minds: "Never again!" At first the hope which these words implied seemed reasonable enough. No direct danger threatened our shores. If the Government were careful to steer clear of entangling alliances, average Americans thought that it could avoid becoming involved in any future troubles that might arise abroad. In 1919-1920, then, we rejected the task of participating in the postwar political reconstruction of Europe and refused to take responsibility for the execution of the peace settlement. We assumed that in some manner the war-wearied European nations would manage to organize themselves for peace, and we hoped that the League of Nations would become effective even without our participation. Secretary Hughes laid what seemed at the time to be a secure basis for maintenance of peace in the Pacific. Successive Administrations tried to help indirectly by working with the League for disarmament; and our Government joined in a solemn declaration renouncing war as an instrument of national policy. Simultaneously, we let our military machine deteriorate as

3

a part of the general world relaxation and our desire
to economize and pay off the costs of the war.

Then came successive blows. The disarmament
efforts proved a dismal failure. Instead of all-round
disarmament we saw the opposite. The armed dic-
tatorships which arose, and the democracies which
tried to catch up with them, both alike had to mortgage their financial future in the race to arm. The
League of Nations proved inadequate to deal with
the heavy tasks laid upon it and the Briand-Kellogg
Pact became a dead letter.

The cumulative effect of these developments was
to make the American people begin to feel genuinely
alarmed. A great war was no longer the remote
danger it once had seemed. It had become a very
real and very threatening possibility. We were not
prepared to do anything very concrete to make it
less likely; in fact, it was not easy to see just what
we could do, except to carry forward Secretary
Hull's persistent efforts to create a more normal
psychology by restoring world trade to its usual
channels. The "Never again" philosophy still was
the dominating influence with the American public,
and the counsel which it gave was still the same—
that the country insulate itself in every way possible from the dangers appearing on several horizons
in Europe, Africa and the Far East.

Towards the end of 1934 and early in 1935,
however, the public began to fear that a simple deter-

mination to remain out of foreign wars might not prove sufficient to preserve American neutrality. Already a discussion had begun in certain private circles as to whether new safeguards might be devised—and, if so, what. Congress and the State Department both became interested. This was the opening of the great debate on neutrality policy. On the one side, in general, have been found those who are anxious to ascertain possible ways of barring activities by our own citizens and of mitigating actions by foreign states which might involve the United States in foreign wars; but they favor doing this only to the extent that the legal steps proposed would be applicable and helpful in all contingencies and would not handicap the Executive in conducting foreign policy so as best to protect the long-range interests of the United States. On the other side, roughly, have been found those who are taken with the idea that peace can be maintained by legislative fiat in all circumstances short of an actual invasion of American soil by foreign troops; they not merely are unconcerned over the possibility that the Executive might not be able to put the weight of the American Government on the side of world peace, but are definitely anxious to curb its actions or endeavors in that direction.

Many books have been written on neutrality in its historical and legal aspects. In these pages we do not propose to deal with the subject from either point of view. The historical neutrality which nations have attempted to maintain almost from the days of chivalry has little practical significance in a world where wars are fought as they are fought today. The legalistic conception of neutrality, and particularly of neutral rights, is based on precedents which had long been confused and weakened by the successively different and inconsistent positions which nations had taken, depending upon whether they expected to be or happened to be neutrals or belligerents. During the World War an American asked an eminent English authority why, when the Declaration of London was being elaborated in 1909, England, reversing her traditional position, favored curtailing the right of a belligerent to interfere with neutral shipping. The answer was: "We expected to be neutral in the next war." And how often we ourselves found in 1914-1917, when we wanted to make good some argument against British trade restrictions, that Great Britain was only taking a leaf out of the book of our own Civil War policies. Final blows to many of the legal formulæ of neutrality were delivered in the World War, and those which remained were further complicated by the changes in the relationship of belligerent and neutral produced by the Covenant of the League of Nations and by the Briand-Kellogg Pact.

Almost any policy of neutrality will serve in a minor conflict. But the policy which the American

Government adopts when the great sea Powers of the world are combatants is of overwhelming importance—for by it may ultimately be decided the question of peace or war, involving the comfort, happiness and perhaps the lives of innumerable American citizens. Our purpose, then, is to make a realistic and non-technical examination of the position of the United States, in the hope of contributing to the study of the alternative courses of action open to our Government in times like the present when the nations of the world with which it has close relations go to war.

We are often reminded that in 1914 we were unprepared for war. By this is generally meant that we were not ready in a military way to uphold our rights promptly in the face of any serious challenge. This is true, at least with regard to the enforcement of our will overseas. But looking back we see now that our lack of preparedness was not military only. We were not prepared as a neutral with any policy which held out a reasonable hope that we could remain safely aside in a protracted conflict between great protagonists. Popular opinion and to some extent official opinion were deluded with the idea that there was a well-defined and accepted status known as "neutrality," and that if we obeyed certain rules known to the initiate, even if not to the man in the street, we could keep out of war. We further expected that, with certain minor restrictions, we could continue to enjoy normal liberties of travel and trade. We had no way of foretelling the scope and application of the new methods and instruments of warfare in ruthless hands. We could not foresee the "war zones" on the high seas, the sowing of mines on the open seas, the unrestricted submarine warfare, or other unprecedented actions which largely did away with the geographical limitations on war. Nor did we foresee the criminal acts of violence on our own territory. Despite our known deficiencies in military equipment, we felt in 1914 that in almost any contingencies our economic strength would force even from belligerents a respect for what we conceived to be our rights.

The experience of the period 1914-1917 should have brought us to an earlier awakening. After the war we should have begun more promptly to examine the problems facing us as a would-be neutral in some other war. Unfortunately, during the decade and a half following "the war that was to end wars" the country was under the spell of the philosophy that the world had "learnt its lesson" and that serious threats to world peace had been eliminated, at least for the lifetime of those who had survived. We were busy recouping our losses and planning new commercial and scientific triumphs. In many circles it was considered indelicate to speak of war as a possibility. As far as our relations with the rest of the world were concerned, many felt that the only task was to consolidate more fully the peace which had been won, and that sufficient means to this end could be found in the limitation and control of armaments, Briand-Kellogg Pacts, *ad hoc* collaboration with other nations on specific issues, and the friendly if not very precise attitude called the policy of "the good neighbor."

What happened in Manchuria was a shock and a warning. The Ethiopian crisis again brought us up short. And not merely did we see two of the seven major Powers of the world deliberately engaging in hostilities. We began to receive warnings from the leader of one of the others that he was merely biding the propitious moment to take whatever he decided his country required, peacefully if nobody opposed, but if necessary by force.

These and other developments brought home to us the need for a clearer conception of our position. The Ethiopian crisis provided the incentive for us to begin thinking out a new policy of neutrality. We should be grateful that the opportunity for debate and experiment came in a situation which had not yet assumed the proportions of a world disaster. But we made a cardinal error in assuming that future wars would all resemble the Italo-Ethiopian war, and in imagining that if we legislated with that particular situation in view we would have provided a satisfactory basis for dealing with other conflicts involving entirely different problems

and presenting different dangers. Later, in the case
of the war in Spain we made the same erroneous
assumption.

It would be a mistake to brush aside the neutrality problem today in an easy belief that the aversion
to war now widely expressed in this country repre-
sents a fixed and permanent attitude. There also
was aversion to war on the eve of our momentous
decisions of 1812 and 1917. The present feeling
plainly is sincere. But to believe that it necessarily
will be lasting is to believe that the present genera-
tion of Americans differs fundamentally from preceding generations. War still retains a certain
amount of glamour for those who have not seen it
close and plain. That we feel strong does not mean
that we have yet reached the degree of detachment
and self-restraint suggested by the phrase "too proud
to fight." We will not tolerate being flouted. In
the future as in the past, we will presumably hold to
what we believe to be our rights; and we will fight
to maintain them if it is necessary. Nor must we
underrate the effect of sincere convictions strongly
held. Many persons will feel that certain fundamental principles of civilization are at stake in any
conflict between great nations, especially when ideo-
logical concepts are involved; and others will see the
long-range interests of the United States menaced by
the impending victory of one side or the other. We

really are no more immune to war fever than any other nation. Indeed, for a country so isolated geographically we have indulged in more than our share of wars. Our press is free; but some of the most widely-read organs have been known to appeal to prejudice, low instincts and the mob spirit. The best we can hope to secure from any neutrality policy is to avoid as many as possible of the incidents that might arouse public feeling, and in the pursuit of this aim to avoid the assertion of rights which are not well-founded and fundamental, and which, once asserted, might involve our national honor and prestige.

The popular American conception that neutrality is a clearly defined status is erroneous. On the contrary, we shall come closer to a correct view if we think of neutrality merely as a policy which, within certain limits, has an almost infinite number of permutations and combinations. As a neutral, we can adopt a policy which indirectly but none the less substantially influences the course of hostilities between other nations by making the American reservoir of goods and raw materials available to those contestants who can receive them; or we can withdraw from commerce where the risk seems too great, as Jefferson tried to do in the early days of the nineteenth century. We can insist on certain so-called neutral rights as we did during the World

War; or we can waive those rights, as many of the European neutrals were forced to do during the same period.

We are often told by eminent counsellors to adopt a "sane" neutrality or a "strict" neutrality or an "impartial" neutrality. All the terms are equally meaningless. No two authorities can agree on a definition of the precise rights and duties of neutrals, except as regards specific and for us minor matters such as the withholding of direct aid by a neutral government to a belligerent, or the duty of a neutral government to refuse to allow its territory to be used as a base for military operations against a belligerent. The trade rights of a neutral are as broad as the power the neutral is willing and able to assert to maintain those rights. If it is unable or unwilling to exert power, those rights are wholly at the mercy of the belligerent and exist only in so far as the belligerent does not find it expedient to curtail them. In fact, they are not rights at all in the sense that we speak of rights in domestic law, where there are courts and impartial agencies for enforcement.

The time has come to stop talking about the alleged virtues of neutrality as such and to turn our attention to the concrete question of planning the general policy which promises to be most expedient for the country to follow now that war has broken out between several Great Powers. We want to stay

out. To this end legislation may help in certain particulars. But we should restrict general legislative
enactments to general and recurring situations, and
deal with the special problems arising out of this
particular conflict by *ad hoc* legislation. Before the
war began we were unable to foresee just what states
would be involved, just what they would be fighting
for, or just how their actions would affect us. In
those circumstances, some of the legislation adopted
can only be called reckless. Today we still cannot
speak with certainty about later phases of the conflict. Nor can we foresee the course of possible
future conflicts. The best we can do is to get some
general principles clearly in mind and determine to
stick to them as long as they serve our national interests. Only so will we be dealing with the realities
of the modern world and escape from the futile
task of furbishing up some old concept of a law of
neutrality as dead as Caesar, with only a ghost to
haunt us.

In the following pages, then, we shall continue
to use the word "neutrality." But it is used in the
sense of *that policy which a country at peace adopts
toward countries at war.* It will not be used as con-
noting a status defined under international law.

Wingate College Library

CHAPTER II

EARLY TESTS OF OUR
NEUTRALITY POLICY

OUR thinking has progressed since 1914. We have come to realize better than we did then that our neutrality policy should be shaped with a view to keeping us out of war rather than toward building up machinery to enable us to exact observance of so-called rights of trade. Have we been careful enough, however, not to be misled by the ease of formulating abstract programs for the relinquishment of American rights? Such programs may sound satisfactory enough and may even find wide acceptance—until the shoe begins to pinch. But if in a time of economic stress we actually try to stop a certain class of exports, whether by moral suasion or by embargo, then we will realize that what is theoretically sound as a war-avoidance policy may be quite unacceptable to hard-pressed agricultural or industrial interests. For the United States is not yet an economically independent unit, our prosperity is tied up with the markets of the world, and voluntarily to step out of international trade may take more fortitude than we possess.

Such, at least, is the lesson to be read in our history—once in the early days when our nation was young and a comparatively unimportant factor in

14

the plans of Europe, once again when we had become a World Power in the full sense of the term.

1. *Neutral Rights and Neutral Duties*

Thomas Jefferson, Secretary of State in Washington's Cabinet, wrote as follows on April 20, 1793, to Gouverneur Morris, the American Minister to France:

> No country perhaps was ever so thoroughly against war as ours. These dispositions pervade every description of its citizens, whether in or out of office. They cannot perhaps suppress their affections nor their wishes. But they will suppress the effects of them so as to preserve a fair neutrality. Indeed, we shall be more useful as neutrals than as parties by the protection which our flag will give to supplies of provision.[1]

Only two months earlier war had broken out between Great Britain and France, the first in a series of conflicts following the French Revolution. With only brief intermissions they continued over a period of twenty-two years and gave the newly established American Government ample opportunity to formulate and test its own policy of neutrality.

Europe seemed so remote in those days of sailing vessels that at first there was little fear that the United States would be drawn into the conflict. Thus Jefferson's note reveals a twofold purpose: not only to keep out of the war, but to continue

[1] P. L. Ford, ed., "The Writings of Thomas Jefferson," v. VI, p. 217.

trading impartially with all the belligerents. Although he abhorred war, Jefferson was quite willing that the United States as a neutral should derive whatever benefits it could from the struggles abroad. "Since it is so decreed by fate," he wrote on hearing rumors of an impending war in Europe, "we have only to pray their soldiers may eat a great deal." In another letter he expressed the hope that "the new world will fatten on the follies of the old."[2]

But since this was a war between maritime powers, there was grave danger that the navies of the belligerents would inflict serious injury on the rapidly growing commerce of the United States. Not only was there danger of the violation of American neutral rights, but there was also danger that foreign agents of the belligerents and their sympathizers in the United States might compromise the country's neutrality through their efforts to assist one or the other of the warring powers. "Citizen" Genet, the new minister from the French Republic, had arrived in the United States soon after the outbreak of war in Europe and proceeded at once to commission privateers to war on British shipping.

This situation prompted President Washington, after a full discussion of the matter with his Cabinet, to issue his neutrality proclamation of April 22,

[2]Quoted in Charles M. Thomas' "American Neutrality in 1793," p. 15-16.

1793. This brief and simply worded document does not even mention the word "neutrality," but it is generally regarded by students of international law as a highly important step in the development of a new phase of the doctrine of neutrality. For instead of emphasizing neutral rights, the proclamation urged that citizens of the United States "should with sincerity and good faith adopt and pursue a conduct friendly and impartial toward the belligerent powers," and "avoid all acts and proceedings whatsoever, which may in any manner tend to contravene such disposition." Americans were warned that by aiding or abetting hostilities against any of the belligerents or "by carrying to any of them those articles which are deemed contraband by the *modern* usage of nations," they would forfeit their rights to the protection of the United States, and that those who violated the law of nations, "within the cognizance of the courts of the United States," would be prosecuted.[3]

The proclamation represented a distinct advance over the previous attitude of other governments toward the duties and obligations of neutrals. And its basic principles have since been generally accepted as the proper code of conduct for non-belligerent nations in time of war. The next step of the American Government was the enactment of a statute conferring authority on Federal officers to

[3]"American State Papers. Foreign Relations," v. I, p. 140.

enforce the policy indicated in President Washington's proclamation. This was accomplished by the Neutrality Act of 1794, which forbade recruiting in the United States for foreign Powers or the fitting out and arming of vessels for service against any belligerent state with which the United States was at peace. The essential features of this measure were embodied in the more inclusive Act of 1818, prescribing what are still the basic principles of the nation's duty as a neutral.

2. *Failure to Keep Out of War in 1812*

The American Government was soon compelled to shift its attention from neutral duties to neutral rights. The European war had not been in progress many months before the British Government, by its Orders in Council, began the seizure of American vessels on the high seas. Great Britain invoked the Rule of War of 1756, by which she had declared that trade which was forbidden to neutrals in time of peace should not be open to them in time of war, and she began seizing vessels trading between the United States and the French West Indies. By an order of November 6, 1793, the British Government directed the seizure of all ships carrying the produce of any French colony or carrying provisions or supplies to such a colony. This order led Congress in March 1794 to impose the first of its embargoes on vessels in American ports planning to sail for foreign ports. This was a temporary embargo and was in effect for only sixty days; but instead of being conducive to peace it seemed to accelerate the drift toward war with Great Britain. A breach with that country was prevented by the Jay Treaty, which though very unpopular was at least a palliative.

The Jay Treaty, however, gave deep offense to France. By the Franco-American Treaty of 1778 France and the United States had already agreed that foodstuffs should not be regarded as contraband and that enemy goods should be safe under a neutral flag. The terms of the Jay Treaty, in the eyes of the French, conflicted with these provisions and were regarded by the French Government as a violation of American neutrality. The French Government thereupon adopted a retaliatory policy, which in 1798 brought the United States into actual, though undeclared, naval war with France. When Napoleon came into power in 1800 some of the differences between the United States and France were adjusted. In March 1802, the European war was stopped for the time being by the Peace of Amiens, and the neutrals obtained a breathing spell. Fourteen months later war broke out afresh and was conducted by both sides with even less regard than before for the rights of neutral nations.

In spite of the depredations on American commerce, the neutrality policy from 1793 to 1805 yielded handsome returns to American citizens; but as encroachments by both belligerents increased, it became more difficult to continue to walk the tight rope. It was impossible for a relatively small and weak nation like the United States of that day effectively to call both offenders to account. Furthermore, Thomas Jefferson, who was now President, was by sentiment a pacifist, and his pacifism took the form of deep resentment against the belligerents for the annoyance caused those who desired to remain at peace. In a letter to Livingston, our newly appointed Minister to France, Jefferson in 1801 set forth his philosophy:

War between two nations cannot diminish the rights of the rest of the world remaining at peace. The doctrine that the rights of nations remaining quietly in the exercise of moral and social duties are to give way to the convenience of those who prefer plundering and murdering one another, is a monstrous doctrine; and ought to yield to the more rational law, that "the wrong which two nations endeavor to inflict on each other, must not infringe on the rights or conveniences of those remaining at peace." And what is *contraband,* by the law of nature? Either everything which may aid or comfort an enemy, or nothing. Either all commerce which would accommodate him is unlawful, or none is. The difference between articles of one or another description, is a difference in degree only. No line between them can be drawn. Either all intercourse must cease between neutrals and belligerents, or all be permitted. Can the world hesitate to say which shall be the rule? Shall two nations turning tigers, break up in one instant the peaceable relations of the whole world? Reason and nature clearly pronounce that the neutral is to go on in the enjoyment of all its rights, that its commerce remains free, not subject to the jurisdiction of another, nor consequently its vessels to search, or to inquiries whether their contents are the property of an enemy, or are of those which have been called contraband of war.[4]

Unfortunately this is a picture of the world as it should be rather than of the world as it is. Jefferson's analysis of the unreality of the rule about contraband is almost prophetic; but his belief that the "rights" of the neutrals must prevail over the "necessity" of the belligerents was as unjustified in the early part of the nineteenth century as similar beliefs proved to be a hundred years later. Jefferson himself was soon to become the unfortunate victim of this discovery. Finding that the nations at war did infringe on the rights and conveniences of those remaining at peace, he still believed that commercial retaliation if applied impartially might compel the belligerent to listen to his protests and at the same time permit the country to remain basically neutral. The outcome was the Embargo Act of December 22, 1807, which has been called a "grand experiment in pacifism." It failed to work as Jefferson had hoped and brought him only chagrin and disappointment.

The embargo did not bring Great Britain and France to accept the American idea of neutrality, but it cut our exports from $108,000,000 (the

[4]"The Works of Thomas Jefferson." Federal Edition, v. IX, p. 299.

abnormal war-profiteering high) to $22,000,000.[5]
It provoked Napoleon to retaliate by ordering the
seizure of all American vessels found in ports under
French jurisdiction, on the pretext that he was aiding the American Government in the suppression of
unlawful commerce.   It created such intense economic disturbance in New England—where it was
openly violated—that secession was openly discussed.
And it finally aroused such opposition throughout
the whole country, and was so difficult to enforce,
that a Congress controlled by Jefferson's own party
repealed it in the last month of his term.   The
Embargo Act was replaced by the Non-Intercourse
Act permitting trade with all countries except Great
Britain and France.   The President was authorized
to resume commercial relations with whichever of
these countries should first remove its restrictions
against American trade.   Napoleon took advantage
of this stipulation.   He revoked certain of his decrees; but this was a pretense, because he gave secret
orders for the seizure of every American ship found
in the ports under his control.

Thereupon, on May 1, 1810, Congress repealed
the Non-Intercourse Act but stipulated that if either
the British or the French Government should revoke
its orders and decrees affecting American trade, the
United States would prohibit commerce with the

[5]John Dickinson, "Neutrality and Commerce." *Proceedings of
the American Society of International Law,* April 25-27, 1935, p. 112.

country still adhering to such restrictions. This measure further encouraged Napoleon to continue his efforts to convince the United States Government that he had in fact revoked his objectionable decrees and hence that it should suspend commercial relations with Great Britain.

As a result of the continued attacks on American commerce by Great Britain and France, a "war party" steadily gained strength in Congress. The United States had equally good reasons for declaring war against either of the belligerents. Napoleon's tortuous course was perhaps even worse than Britain's frank disregard of our neutral rights; but the offenses committed by Great Britain were the greater in quantity, due to her increasing control of the seas. In consequence, public resentment was greatest against the British. On June 1, 1812, President Madison sent a message to Congress declaring that Great Britain had abandoned "all respect for the neutral rights of the United States," and on June 18 Congress made a formal declaration of war. The policy of attempted insulation had been tried and found wanting.

CHAPTER III

NEUTRALITY FAILS IN 1917

IN THE opening decade of the twentieth century, unbeknownst to many Americans, the United States had become a World Power. In 1908 it was still possible for a book by a distinguished historian to attract unusual attention merely because its title recognized the fact.[1]

The country's foreign trade had been growing by leaps and bounds; by 1913 exports reached a value of nearly two and a half billion dollars. Exports which bulked so large in the national economy naturally exercised a correspondingly important political influence at Washington. Today we tend to forget this fact. In the last two decades the American export trade has been changing drastically in character, and its influence has changed with it. Our cotton exports have decreased roughly from 8,500,000 bales in 1913 to 5,440,000 bales in 1937, and our wheat and flour exports have decreased from 155,000,000 bushels in 1913 to 21,000,000 bushels in 1937. Since cotton and wheat are commodities which play a chief rôle in American politics, our foreign trade had far more political significance in 1914 than it has today. Now it is the indus-

[1] "The United States as a World Power," by Archibald Cary Coolidge, was the first comprehensive survey of the country's new international position.

trialists who have the biggest stake in our trade
with other nations; automobile makers, oil producers
and others often exercise an important influence on
domestic legislation; but their interest in general
policies is not homogeneous and, due to the fact that
a sparsely settled agricultural state has as many
Senators as a populous industrial one, has not yet
proved so effective politically as has the interest of
the agrarian bloc.[2]

This digression has been introduced merely to
indicate that in viewing the factors which led us to
adopt a vigorous policy in defense of trade in the
opening phases of the World War we must take
account of the different conditions then existing. Of
course we must not imagine that today our cotton
growers or our farmers have abandoned hope of re-
gaining some of their lost foreign markets or that
they would not resist measures which deprived them
of any part of the export trade that still remains.
Nevertheless, the demand on the Government that
it actively protect foreign trade menaced on the high
seas by foreign acts of war has distinctly less political support than twenty-five years ago.

We have already suggested that we were unprepared as a people and as a government to deal with
the conditions created by a general European war.

[2]Though our exports of manufactured goods are less than they
were in the boom days of 1929, they nevertheless are higher than they
were twenty-five years ago. The changes in the composition of American foreign trade from 1913 to 1937 are shown in Appendix 16.

There was no time in the summer of 1914 to sit down quietly to weigh the consequences of alternative courses to meet a situation which daily became more complicated, much less to think out a long-range policy. All that our Government could do was cling to the best precedents available, even though second thought might have raised doubts as to whether they really were applicable to the new conditions of maritime warfare, especially when such mighty antagonists were involved. We stuck to the precedents; and they led us step by step nearer the arena.

It became rather the fashion with American writers a few years ago to "debunk" the history of our period of neutrality and of our entry at last into the war in 1917. The procedure may have had its uses, but it was carried too far and produced some serious misconceptions in the public mind. Thus the impression was given by certain influential books that the United States was caught in the World War primarily because of the preponderance of British propaganda, the subtleties of British diplomacy, and the influence of vested financial, commercial and industrial interests whose fortunes became tied up with an Allied victory. These factors all counted. But to single them out and stress them heavily seems to us to allow too little for the natural predisposition of many Americans for certain principles and their antipathy for certain others

—for what Winston Churchill has called "the rhythm of tragedy," the cumulative effect on the public conscience of that vast interplay of fact and sentiment from the day the German armies crossed the Belgian frontier in August 1914 with the watchword "necessity knows no law," until President Wilson, addressing the Senate on April 2, 1917, set a public seal on his reluctant decision: "The present German submarine warfare against commerce is a warfare against mankind. It is a war against all nations."

The tendency of much of this literature is to ignore the fundamental reasons why American sentiment turned in favor of the Allies and against Germany. Thus one looks in vain in Walter Millis' interesting volume, "Road to War," for a reference to the fact that there was a treaty guaranteeing Belgium, that Germany had signed it, and that Germany's violation of it exercised an instantaneous and persistent effect on American feeling toward Germany. The Belgian deportations are called an "attack upon the unemployment problem in Belgium and Northern France;" it is not mentioned that in 1917 Germany ordered the stoppage of all public works undertaken by the Belgian communes and provinces for the relief of unemployment, that she had already removed to Germany many of the instruments and machines of labor, that the forced labor to which the deportees were condemned was

work for the enemy, often on military roads and
trenches near the front, that hence the Belgians
were willing to suffer punishment and go into exile
rather than work, and that many Americans pitied
and applauded them.   When Mr. Millis describes
the staff of the American Legation in Brussels and
the American correspondents as naïve for not emphasizing that Belgian *francs tireurs* were technically guilty of atrocities in sniping at the invading
troops, and that the German high command was technically justified in lining up local hostages and shoot-
ing them, he misses the point; no emphasis on the
illegality of the Belgian civilian action or the legality
of the German military reprisals would have made
the American public of that day feel that the Belgian
defenders were not acting heroically and justifiably
and that the German invaders were not acting in a
contrary sense.   Other cases could be cited in this
volume, and in others, of a failure to appreciate the
origins of the sentiment which as the war developed
played an important part in shaping American
policy.   For example, the hostile and criminal acts
of German agents in the United States irritated the
public much more than is now remembered, and the
public placed them in a different category from the
propaganda and publicity work of Allied writers and
lecturers.   It seems to the present authors unrealistic to imagine that deep-rooted sentiment can be
dismissed as an important factor in determining the

policies of nations. And perhaps it is unjustified to
assume that the elimination of sentiment—some
might call it devotion to principle, others might term
it mere prejudice—is necessarily desirable, even
though one can prove that in specific cases it might
well be.

We do not think one has to search either in Wall
Street or Downing Street for a Machiavelli to ex-
plain the American attitude in 1914-1917. Whatever may have been the effect of hired propaganda
or the influence of financial and commercial interests, they do not fully account for our intervention.

What really happened, we believe, was that from
the very beginning of the war American sympathies
were engaged. On top of that, and of decisive importance, the course which the Government took in
demanding observance of its traditional neutral
rights engaged the national honor of the United
States in the defense of the principle that its trade
should continue and that its nationals were entitled
to protection in the exercise of that trade. When
those rights were curtailed by Great Britain, we
protested. When our citizens who were exercising
those rights were killed by Germany, when our ships
were sunk, and when Germany formally challenged
our asserted rights through the unrestricted submarine campaign, then we went to war. If our basic
policy in insisting on our full neutral rights was
sound, what other course in self-respect could we

have followed?[3]   Whether or not the conception was
sound is the question to consider.

Upon the outbreak of war we started out with
the idea that there must be certain inherent rights
of trade, a thesis which we had consistently maintained throughout our history.   Like his predeces-
sors—Washington, Adams, Jefferson and Madison
—President Wilson was soon engaged in the effort
to keep out of war, maintain neutrality, and at the
same time make good the illusive and indefinite doctrine known as the Freedom of the Seas.   But now
there was no serious question of embargoes or non-
intercourse as in the days of Jefferson.   Trade was
too important.   To be sure, when Congress met in
December 1914, bills were introduced to embargo
the export of arms and munitions, one of them sponsored by an important Democrat, Senator Hitchcock
of Nebraska.   The influences which prevented its
adoption were not primarily commercial.   The
Hitchcock Bill suffered from being presented as a
humanitarian measure rather than as a move to keep
us out of the war, and it was attacked (and defeated) as preparing an "unneutral" change in our
laws after a foreign conflict had begun.[4]   Neverthe-

[3]Count Bernstorff, German Ambassador at Washington, in a statement issued to the press immediately after being handed his passports
on February 3, 1917, said: "I am not surprised.   My government will
not be surprised either.   The people in Berlin knew what was bound
to happen if they took the action they have taken.   There was nothing
else left for the United States to do."   ("War Memoirs of Robert
Lansing," p. 217.)

[4]*Cf.* Walter Millis, "Road to War: America, 1914-1917."

less, the fact that our people had never doubted their right and ability to continue trade with belligerents and still remain neutral, and the fact that the relinquishment of that trade would have played havoc with many fundamental American occupations, were root causes of our whole attitude.

As a legal basis for the position which we assumed regarding trade we first tried to make use of the Declaration of London of 1909, which defined contraband, blockade, etc. With all its defects, it would have served as a useful statement of what we then hoped was the international law on the subject. Great Britain, however, had never ratified the Declaration of London and refused to apply it without modifications which we felt deprived it of its real value.[5]

Lord Grey commented as follows upon the Declaration of London:

Had it been in full force its rules would have hampered us in some respects, particularly in the list of contraband, at the outset of the war; and those who opposed and defeated it are entitled on this account to take credit for their action. Whether, if the Declaration had been ratified and observed as a whole by the belligerents, the balance of advantage and

[5]In passing, we may note that the Declaration of London was a treaty solemnly negotiated in the British capital, approved and signed by the British delegates, and accepted by the House of Commons. Due to its rejection by the House of Lords, it was never ratified by the British Government. Thus though it was approved by the United States Senate it of course was never put into effect by the President. The United States is thus not the only Power which has failed to ratify the signature of its negotiators to an important treaty.

disadvantage would have been in our favor or not is a different question, and one less easy to answer. If it had prevented the submarine war on merchant vessels, it would have saved us from our greatest peril in the war. To this it may be replied that, but for the German submarine war on merchant vessels, the United States would not have come in on the side of the Allies.

The question is not worth pursuing: if the Declaration had been ratified, it would have been broken. The same ruthless spirit that introduced the use of poison-gas, an offense not only against rules of war but against all humane considerations, would have made short work of the Declaration of London.[6]

When the Declaration of London had to be abandoned we fell back upon what we claimed to be the recognized rules of international law. But in doing so we had to recognize that international law failed to give us a definite code and that this failure would "undoubtedly be the source of numerous controversies."[7] Further, particularly in our dealings with the British, the doctrines we had maintained in the Civil War came in to plague us. We had ourselves broadened the idea of "continuous voyage," the doctrine under which we seized goods which were en route to a neutral port but which we asserted had an ultimate enemy destination; and we had extended the list of contraband. In writing to Senator Stone on January 20, 1915, Secretary of State Bryan admitted:

[6]Lord Grey, "Twenty-five Years, 1892-1916," v. 2, pp. 105-6.
[7]"Woodrow Wilson: Life and Letters," v. 5, p. 218.

The record of the United States in the past is not free from criticism. When neutral, this Government has stood for a restricted list of absolute and conditional contraband. As a belligerent, we have contended for a liberal list, according to our conception of the necessities of the case.

In the same letter, in discussing the trade with neutral ports, Secretary Bryan added:

It will be recalled, however, that American courts have established various rules bearing on these matters. The rule of "continuous voyage" has been not only asserted by American tribunals but extended by them.[8]

But even more serious than these admissions was our recognition in an early communication to Great Britain,

that the commerce between countries which are not belligerents should not be interfered with by those at war unless such interference is manifestly an imperative necessity to protect their national safety, and then only to the extent that is is a necessity.[9]

It did not take the British long to reach the conclusion that the suppression of our trade with Germany was an imperative necessity. As Lord Grey stated,

the object of [British] diplomacy, therefore, was to secure the maximum of blockade that could be enforced without a rupture with the United States.

[8]Papers Relating to the Foreign Relations of the United States," 1914, Supplement, The World War, p. ix.

[9]Cable of Secretary Bryan to Ambassador Page, December 26, 1914, *ibid.*, p. 373.

Simultaneously with the interruption of our trade with Germany another phenomenon occurred. Our trade with the Allies grew to a point where it more than took the place of the German trade. Thus the domestic political and economic effect of the British blockade, except in certain limited circles, was not enduring. The international consequences were, however, portentous.

The United States took a position which was logical and which fitted both the sentimental and the national interests of the country, namely that we were under no duty arbitrarily to rectify the consequences of British control of the sea. We would trade where we could, and thus fill the gaps caused by the loss of trade with Germany, whose ports, as well as the ports of neighboring countries, were largely closed to us as a result of the extension of the contraband list and the doctrine of continuous voyage. Further, we considered it objectionable as a matter of principle to change what we conceived to be the rules of neutrality during the course of the war. Thus Secretary Bryan wrote to Count von Bernstorff on April 21, 1915:

. . . any change in its own laws of neutrality during the progress of a war which would affect unequally the relations of the United States with the nations at war would be an unjustifiable departure from the principles of strict neutrality.[10]

[10]"Papers Relating to the Foreign Relations of the United States," 1915, Supplement, The World War, p. 162.

The answer was Germany's submarine challenge to British sea power. In the face of this the legal precedents to which we were clinging seemed more secure. There were no serious Civil War precedents to embarrass us in protesting against the illegalities of submarine warfare, for submarines had not then been invented. Further, in that war the lives of civilians whether on neutral or belligerent merchant vessels had been generally safeguarded, again largely because the submarine did not yet exist.

When, therefore, Germany in February 1915 proclaimed that the waters surrounding Great Britain were to be considered within the seat of war our answer was the "strict accountability" note. We stated in that note that

the Government of the United States would be constrained to hold the Imperial German Government to a strict accountability for such acts of their naval authorities and to take any steps it might be necessary to take to safeguard American lives and property and to secure to American citizens the full enjoyment of their acknowledged rights on the high seas.[11]

There, in a few words, is the thesis which, logically pursued, led to war. It was stated before the blossoming of the "war boom" based on trade with the Allies, and seven months before the first Allied public loan in this country. We were insisting on what we claimed to be full enjoyment of *acknowl-*

[11]*Ibid.*, p. 99.

edged rights. In a note to Germany a few months later the same idea appears:

> The rights of neutrals in time of war are based upon principle, not upon expediency, and the principles are immutable. It is the duty and obligation of belligerents to find a way to adapt the new circumstances to them.[12]

This might have been Jefferson speaking in 1801. If we meant what we said, war would become inevitable whenever, weighing the advantages and disadvantages of adding us to the list of her enemies, Germany felt impelled to act contrary to these "immutable principles" and "acknowledged rights." True, we had admitted the law of necessity in our earlier notes to Great Britain where trade only was involved; but we did not recognize that the law of necessity could be invoked to justify putting the lives of our citizens in jeopardy. Said Secretary Lansing on June 9, 1915:

> But the sinking of passenger ships involves principles of humanity which throw into the background any special circumstances of detail that may be thought to affect the cases. .... The Government of the United States is contending for something much greater than mere rights of property or privileges of commerce. It is contending for nothing less high and sacred than the rights of humanity, which every Government honors itself in respecting and which no Government is justified in resigning on behalf of those under its care and authority.[13]

[12]*Ibid.,* p. 481.

[13]*Ibid.,* p. 437.

These grave words, and the acts to which they were the prelude, should be a lesson to us that in the last analysis it is the attack on human life, rather than the attack on property interest, which is most likely to set in motion the tides of resentment which can impel a country like the United States into war. It is more important as a war-prevention measure for us to avoid incidents which might involve the lives of our citizens than to curtail trade relationships, provided it is possible to maintain the latter without risk to American lives.

There is no doubt that President Wilson was entirely sincere in his desire to maintain neutrality. "The United States," he said on August 19, 1914, "must be neutral in fact as well as in name during these days that are to try men's souls. We must be impartial in thought as well as in action, must put a curb upon our sentiments as well as upon every transaction that might be construed as a preference of one party to the struggle before another."[14] This represented a slight development, however, from the general position of "impartial neutrality" which was urged in his proclamation of two weeks earlier. That proclamation stated flatly that "the full expression of sympathies in public and in private is not restricted by the laws of the United States."

[14]The full text of President Wilson's Proclamation of Neutrality, August 4, 1914, and of his Statement of August 19, 1914, is given in Appendix 1 and Appendix 2.

Theodore Roosevelt in September 1914 thought it "eminently desirable" to remain neutral. It was not until some months later that he accused Wilson of "poltroonery" for not having protested the invasion of Belgium. His change of mind is not attributable mainly to political motives, though a love of political invective undoubtedly played a part. What happened to him happened to many other Americans, some sooner, some later. They saw a battle royal in progress, and in their hearts they took sides. Then, as the position which our Government had taken from the very outset produced the material and legal grounds for participation, feeling and fact coalesced; we participated.

Today we must recognize that when President Wilson engaged our national honor and prestige in the defense of "rights" upon the high seas and at the same time tried to maintain neutrality he was waging a losing fight. Moreover, two parallel developments were making his task no easier. As noted above, the American public were coming to like German military behavior less and less, and were beginning more and more to speculate whether their own vital interests were not menaced by the possibility of a German victory. And in President Wilson's own heart and mind, where he had struggled so hard to maintain "impartial neutrality," there began to grow, following the failure of his negotiations with Germany in the opening weeks of 1917, a conviction that he was dealing with a ruthless military force and that its political spokesmen either were impotent or thoroughly untrustworthy. With the commencement of unrestricted German submarine sinkings on February 1, 1917, the final bitter conviction gripped him that western civilization faced a crisis in which he personally could no longer remain detached. It was only nine weeks from Germany's resolution to "sink at sight" to our entry into the war.

The plain fact is that our sentiments are likely to become engaged in almost any great and prolonged conflict. It may happen because we feel that our national honor is injured by flagrant attacks on a legal position which our Government has deliberately adopted and persistently maintained—and especially, of course, if these attacks result in the loss of American lives. Or it may happen, even without a direct attack, because our people and their leaders sense some menace to certain general principles about which they care deeply and the preservation of which in the modern world seems to them important. Or, as in 1917, the two streams of reason and feeling may fuse in a determination to resist, if need be by force.

Possibly this characteristic reveals our naïveté. Or possibly it is to our credit. In any event it is an American characteristic of long standing. We cannot rely for the maintenance of neutrality on the calm of our press and people. Any grave incident which seemed to involve our national honor or seemed seriously to menace our ability to continue living our lives in the traditional American way would find us again ready to fight, despite our devotion to peace in the abstract and despite the activities of peace societies or isolationist senators and congressmen. What we should plan to do, if our principal desire is to avoid war, is not to let our national honor get tied up with the exercise abroad, in war zones, of any preconceived rights which are not in fact essential to our national existence, and not to let hasty sentiment overpower reason in a just appraisal of our long-range interests.

CHAPTER IV

FROM COLLECTIVE SECURITY BACK TO NEUTRALITY

A MERICANS have a strong feeling for peace, even though they may be vague about just what it is and about how best to maintain it. They are progressive and scientifically minded and they like to think that their approach to the problems of the machine age is realistic. But they have been slow to grasp the transformations which scientific discovery, industrialization and the development of communications have made in society and in international relationships. The feeling of continental security and of aloofness from Europe had been dominant in the United States for so long that when the World War was over the public were predisposed toward accepting the idea that they had blundered into it or been manœuvred into it, and that they could easily stay out of similar entanglements in the future if only their government would mind its own business.

Naturally enough, then, during the fifteen years immediately following the World War the public gave little thought to our possible troubles as a neutral in hypothetical future conflicts. But there were other and even more cogent reasons for our lack of attention to this question. The Senate's defeat of the Treaty of Versailles did not mean that we broke completely with the system for the preservation of peace which that Treaty had set up and which the European Powers were endeavoring to implement. Our refusal to ratify the Treaty only meant that we proposed to adopt an independent course in correlating American action with that of the Treaty Powers, and did not exclude the possibility that our action in many particulars would parallel theirs. Neutrality in the old sense was quite pushed into the background.

It is often forgotten today that during this period the United States made a real effort to help build up an international order in which neutrality in the old legalistic sense would become an outmoded concept. The transition from idealistic conceptions of what was called collective security back to cold realities was gradual. For over a decade we did our best to bring about disarmament, starting with the Washington Conference of 1921-1922 and ending with the Disarmament Conference which collapsed in 1934. During these discussions our Government clearly indicated that if a disarmament treaty could be concluded we might consider a change in our position as a neutral. At Geneva on May 22, 1933, Norman H. Davis made the following statement at a session of the Disarmament Conference:

". . . I wish to make it clear that we are ready not only to do our part toward the substantive reduction of armaments but, if this is effected by general international agreement, we are also prepared to contribute in other ways to the organization of peace. In particular, we are willing to consult with other states in case of a threat to peace, with a view of averting conflict. Further than that, in the event that the states, in conference, determine that a state has been guilty of a breach of the peace in violation of its international obligations and take measures against the violator, then, if we concur in the judgment rendered as to the responsible and guilty party, we will refrain from any action tending to defeat such collective effort which the states may thus make to restore peace."

Several years earlier, in 1928, we had entered into the Briand-Kellogg Pact, by which the signatories agreed with each other not to settle differences between them by force. This also implied a change in our position as a neutral. For the first time in our history we put ourselves in a situation where we had a legal right to interest ourselves in any war, since war anywhere among the nations which had signed the Briand-Kellogg Pact would presumably involve a violation of a treaty to which we were a party. As late as August 1932, Henry L. Stimson, Secretary of State, reminded the country in an important pronouncement of governmental policy that the Briand-Kellogg Pact had altered the relations of nations. He said that as a result of the Pact war had become "an illegal thing." And he continued:

"Hereafter when two nations engage in armed conflict either one or both of them must be wrongdoers —violators of the general treaty. We no longer draw a circle about them and treat them with the punctilios of the duelist's code. Instead we denounce them as lawbreakers. By that very act we have made obsolete many legal precedents and have given the legal profession the task of reëxamining many of its codes and treaties."[1]

The outbreak of trouble in Manchuria, and the withdrawal of Japan and then of Germany from the League of Nations, were warning signals to us that the collective system was tottering. At last by 1934 we began to realize fairly clearly that we could no longer rely upon the universal acceptance of a new code in international relations. Wars of the old type threatened, though they might employ new weapons. There were still problems for neutrals to face, greater problems, perhaps, than ever. It was then that the Administration realized the need of beginning a serious and detailed study of what to do in case the general treaty safeguards to world peace should fail. The effort to strengthen those safeguards did not altogether cease; but attention shifted more and more to the task of developing a program of action in the contingency that war broke out between two or more powerful na-

[1]Speech before the Council on Foreign Relations, New York, August 8, 1932. (*Foreign Affairs,* v. 11, no. 1, Supplement.)

tions. If that happened, the United States might be called upon to choose suddenly, in the light of its past experience—and particularly its experience between 1914 and 1917—which of its traditional rights were vital and could and should be defended to the uttermost, and which were unessential and might be relinquished if by so doing we could remain at peace.

There were other problems, too, resulting from the development of new methods and machines of war in the air and under the sea, the adoption of new means of communication and propaganda, and the alterations which science had made in the economic capabilities and needs of various nations. All these affected vitally the position of the United States as a World Power and had a bearing on its ability to remain outside disputes originating in other continents. All, therefore, had to be taken into consideration in mapping a new neutrality program.

In a memorable article published in *Foreign Affairs* in April 1934 Mr. Charles Warren set out to answer some of the questions involved. Mr. Warren had been Assistant Attorney-General in the Wilson Administration and had wrestled with the legal aspects of the neutrality problem prior to our entry into the World War. He now drew on his unique experience to list the points where the position of the United States seemed particularly exposed, and where he thought legislation was needed in order to lessen the risk of fresh embroilment in foreign wars. Mr. Warren did not minimize the price which the American people would have to pay to remain neutral. He was not sanguine that the price might not seem to them too high; and he consequently drew the moral that their first interest and duty should be to reconsider the question of joining with other nations in any practicable step to prevent the occurrence of war, so as to avoid if possible being forced to choose between the horrid alternatives with which the outbreak of war would certainly face them.

Mr. Warren not long afterwards was invited to assist the Department of State in drawing up a program of neutrality legislation to be sponsored by the Administration; and the McReynolds bill and to some degree the Joint Resolution eventually adopted showed the influence of his views. We therefore may summarize the proposals which he put forward in his article as affording a fairly good outline of what thoughtful persons even at that time realized would have to be done if the United States could hope to make a reasonable effort to remain at peace. Mr. Warren's proposals were that when war breaks out anywhere the American Government shall:

1. Take over control of all high-power radio stations, and forbid the use of radio instruments by any foreign ship in our ports or waters.

2. Forbid the sale of arms and ammunition to belligerents.

3. Even if all such sales are not prohibited, at least prohibit their shipment in American vessels; further, forbid American citizens to travel as passengers or crew on any ship, belligerent or domestic, carrying arms or munitions.

4. Forbid the entrance into our ports of merchantmen armed either for offense or defense; and forbid American citizens to travel on such ships.

5. Close our ports to any ship of a belligerent nation which permits its ships to fly the American flag for purposes of deception.

6. As a preliminary measure, revise present treaties so as to be free to forbid prize ships from being brought into our ports.

7. Bar American ports and waters to all foreign submarines; and forbid the aircraft of belligerent nations to descend on or pass over American territory.

8. Oblige merchant sihps of belligerents in our ports at the outbreak of war to leave within a specified time, on pain of being taken into custody until such time as they desire to clear.

9. Forbid the use of our ports as bases for the supply of food and coal to belligerent warships on the high seas; and in general forbid entrance to our ports and waters of any ship of a belligerent which shall have violated the law of neutrality or our statute laws, as well as forbid clearance to any ship, domestic or foreign, owned by any corporation or person which shall have committed such a violation.

10. Consider merchant ships chartered or requisitioned by belligerent governments as supply ships of their navies, and intern them if they remain in our waters longer than international law allows for belligerent war vessels.

11. Forbid loans to belligerent governments by private citizens.

12. Forbid not only recruitment for belligerent armies, but also the collection here of foreign reservists; and forbid enlistment of American citizens in the armies of belligerent countries.

Mr. Warren further urged at length that in any future major war the United States should not attempt to insist on alleged neutral rights of trade. "It is better," he wrote, "that our citizens should run the risk of commercial loss than that the country should be involved in a war to protect their alleged commercial rights." And he added that "our Government might very properly say, in effect, to its citizens during the war: you engage in such trade at your own risk during the existence of the war, and you can protect your trade by requiring a profit correlative to the risk."

While the Department of State was carrying forward its neutrality studies in 1934 and the early part of 1935, two events, one domestic and the other international, tended to accelerate the pace and accentuate the urgency of the task. Since the spring of 1934 a Senatorial Committee presided over by Senator Nye had been making an investigation of the munitions industry and the international traffic in arms, and in this connection had been delving into the causes of our entry into the World War in 1917. The hearings of the Committee were widely publicized and increased the widespread impression in the public mind that there is something unusually vicious and sinister in the traffic in arms as such. Specifically, the hearings tended to give the impression that the trade in war materials between 1914 and 1917, together with the loans made to finance that trade, had had an important influence in bringing us into the World War. The Committee stated its conclusion in a report published June 16, 1936:

"The Committee finds, on the basis of the testimony and exhibits introduced into the record and discussed in Chapter III, War Trade Expansion, that the development of the export of war commodities to the Allies resulted in a widespread expansion of almost all the lines of American business, an expansion which J. P. Morgan & Co., in their commercial agency contracts, specifically undertook to stimulate. As a result by 1916 there was created a tremendous industrial machine, heavily capitalized, paying high wages, and dependent upon the purchasing power of the Allies. The Committee is of the opinion that this situation, with its risk of business depression and panic in event of damage to the belligerents' ability to purchase, involved the administration so inextricably it prevented the maintenance of a truly neutral course between the Allies and the Central Powers. Such a neutral course threatened to injure this export trade."[1]

[1]74th Congress, 2d sess., Senate Report No. 944, Part 6, p. 3.

WINGATE JUNIOR COLLEGE

The pros and cons of this thesis have been widely debated. The present authors believe (and have given their reasons in a previous chapter) that the influence of munitions profiteers and international bankers has probably been greatly exaggerated as a decisive factor in our intervention in the World War. The fact remains that an impression to this effect gained general credence at about this time, and it must be taken into account when we consider the moment and character of the initial steps taken in Washington to develop new neutrality legislation.

More specifically it was the threat of war in Ethiopia which induced Congress to turn to the extremely complicated and contentious problem of neutrality at the fag end of an acrimonious session and in the torrid summer weather of August 1935. Mussolini's menacing attitude indicated that a war might well be in progress before Congress would reconvene in January 1936; and by common consent, clearly reflected in Congress, the American people wished to have nothing to do with it.

The public's feeling at that time still had about it a good deal of the old conception that peace is a state of mind rather than a condition resulting from a continuing series of positive acts, that it is something bestowed rather than something bought at a price. It still reflected the confusion between the ideas of "isolation" and "safety" which had so

clearly manifested itself during the fight over our
participation in the League of Nations. At the
same time there was still a broad section of our
public which had not yet given up hope that the
League of Nations might even yet make a contribution toward peace, and that if this were the case we
would not want to do anything to increase the difficulties of its task. In the electoral campaign of 1932
President Roosevelt had carried many states usually
considered to be isolationist on a platform which
was not afraid to advocate making the Briand-
Kellogg Pact more effective "by provisions for consultation and conference in case of threatened violation of treaties." Further, in view of the American
Government's prominent part in elaborating the
Briand-Kellogg Pact, nothing seemed more natural
than that the openly avowed intention of a signatory
of that treaty to violate it should produce a pro-
found effect on public opinion in this country and
reinforce the sentiment that the United States
should not remain wholly aloof from efforts by
members of the League to put a stop to the war,
even by the extreme method of imposing sanctions
on the aggressor.

It was in this confused situation—with the
isolationists demanding action; with the coöpera-
tionists similarly pressing for action, though for
quite different motives; and with the Administration
convinced that our neutrality statutes as they had

been applied in the World War were outmoded and inadequate—that Congress adopted in haste, and as a compromise between many contradictory opinions and aims, the first of a series of laws which with modifications and amendments still remain on our statute books to regulate our conduct in time of war.

CHAPTER V

LEGISLATING FOR PEACE

THERE have been four legislative enactments on neutrality since 1935. The first was the Neutrality Act of August 31, 1935. The second was the Joint Resolution amending it, adopted February 29, 1936. The third was the Spanish Arms Embargo Resolution of January 8, 1937. The fourth was the Neutrality Act of May 1, 1937. Examination of this legislation is necessary for a full understanding of the historical background of the current situation. But the procedure will be rather dry, and we give our less conscientious readers a hint to skim through at least the first sections of this chapter.

The various pieces of legislation enumerated above are generally referred to as Neutrality Acts. This is a misnomer, as some of our legislative draftsmen have apparently begun to realize. In fact the abortive neutrality proposal introduced into the Senate by Senator Pittman in March 1939 states in the preamble that it should be referred to as the "Peace Act of 1939." But efforts to popularize laws by giving them appealing labels are not likely to succeed; and to call such legislation either neutrality legislation or peace legislation is misleading.

Certain technical provisions relating chiefly to the treatment of belligerent vessels in our ports fit into the general scheme of our basic neutrality statutes as amended to 1917.[1] Except for these provisions, the legislation adopted in 1935 and revised and amended in succeeding years is primarily legislation to restrict and control American commerce and circumscribe the activities of our citizens in time of war.

This is not said by way of criticism of these laws but merely to put them in their correct light. No abstract conception of neutrality and nothing in the long history of the international law of neutrality requires that a neutral country should place restrictions on the commerce of its nationals, provided this commerce does not take the form of fitting out armed expeditions on neutral territory. In the exercise of our sovereign rights, and within the scope of our constitutional powers to regulate foreign trade, the Government, with Congressional sanction, can impose such restrictions on foreign trade as it may desire. During the Napoleonic Wars it even put an embargo on our foreign trade. The question for our Government to decide is solely and simply whether these restrictions are desirable in our own national interest. No question of fulfilling an international obligation is involved. In fact, it is unfortunate that the United States should have started the precedent of linking restrictions which it sees fit to place on its own trade with its duties as

[1] Published in full in Appendix 4.

a neutral, as occurred when laws such as those which we are discussing were entitled Neutrality Acts. It would be desirable from more than one point of view to change labels and give this legislation its proper title, namely, laws to restrict American commerce in time of war.[2]

The Neutrality Act of 1935

In the spring of 1935, at the unmistakable signs that war was being prepared in Africa and fearing that it might furnish the spark for another European conflagration, the American public was filled with the healthy determination not to become involved. This feeling paralleled a desire on the part of many Americans that if possible we help put a stop to it. As Mussolini's legions poured through Suez, the American people spoke loudly to their representatives at Washington, demanding that they make ready to deal with any contingencies in the impending hostilities. Several members of Congress already had introduced bills designed to safeguard the neutrality of the United States; and as the threat of war increased others appeared, some of them quite drastic. From January 10 to August 17, 1935, no less than five so-called neutrality bills were introduced in the Senate and ten in the House. Some aimed to prohibit loans and credits to belligerents,

[2]If in succeeding pages the legislation of 1935 and subsequent years is referred to as neutrality legislation, this is done only to avoid awkward circumlocutions and to conform to accepted terminology, inaccurate though it be.

some proposed arms embargoes, some covered both questions and others besides.

As has been already described, the Administration had been conducting a study of the whole neutrality problem for over a year. The views of the Department of State were set forth in a bill introduced on August 17, 1935, by Representative McReynolds, Chairman of the House Committee on Foreign Affairs. They have had such an influence on subsequent neutrality discussions that they seem worth summarizing here in some detail. The bill provided in substance as follows:

1. "That upon the outbreak of or during the progress of the war between or among two or more foreign states, or whenever the President finds that conditions existing in any part of the world are such that the shipment of arms, ammunition, and implements of war from the United States may involve the United States in international complications or contribute to armed conflict, and when in either such case the President finds that the imposition of restrictions on the export of such war material from the United States will serve to maintain peace between the United States and foreign nations or to protect the commercial interests of the United States and its citizens or to promote the security of the United States and shall so proclaim, it shall thereafter be unlawful to export arms, ammunition, or implements of war from any place in the United States to such countries as the President may designate."

2. That in similar circumstances, upon proclamation by the President, "it shall be unlawful for any vessel of the

United States to carry any arms, ammunition, or implements of war to any port of a belligerent country, or to any neutral port for transshipment to, or for the use of, a belligerent country."

3. That the use of American ports as bases for belligerent warships be prohibited.

4. That the President be authorized to prohibit entrance to American ports of the vessels of a belligerent nation if he finds that vessels of that nation are using the American flag.

5. That the President be authorized to place special restrictions on the use of American ports by belligerent submarines.

6. That the President be authorized to prohibit loans to belligerents.

7. That the President be authorized to proclaim that travel by American citizens on the vessels of belligerent nations (except under certain specified circumstances) shall be at their own risk.

A majority in the Senate were found to be against giving the President the degree of discretion proposed in this bill. The prevailing Senate view was that to allow the President to discriminate between belligerents was tantamount to allowing him to pick the aggressor, which meant taking sides morally. Some Senators thought that this would be a risky procedure. The Senate did not discuss in detail the second question involved, namely, the effect our stand would have on the League's ability to act effectively against an aggressor.   Nor did the public have a clear understanding on this point.

There was no objection in principle to the idea of an arms embargo, although in the past, prior to the Chaco War, we had used it in instances of internal strife abroad rather than in cases of international warfare.[3]   During the World War we had vigorously insisted upon our right to continue to permit the export of arms, taking the position that to place an embargo on it would constitute a change in our law of neutrality which would be an unjustifiable departure from the principle of strict neutrality.   Secretary Lansing, in reply to an Austro-Hungarian demand that an embargo be placed on "enormous" American exports of munitions to the Allies, wrote on August 12, 1915:

To this assertion of an obligation to change or modify the rules of international usage on account of special conditions the Government of the United States can not accede. . . . Manifestly the idea of strict neutrality now advanced by the Imperial and Royal Government would involve a neutral nation in a mass of perplexities which would obscure the whole field of international obligation, produce economic confusion. . . . During the Boer War between Great Britain and the South African Republics . . . in spite of the commercial isolation of one belligerent, Germany sold to Great Britain, the other belligerent, hundreds of thousands of kilos of explosives, gunpowder, cartridges, shot, and weapons; and it

[3]For a note on previous American arms embargoes, by William O. Scroggs, see Appendix 15.   Also see "The Embargo Resolutions and Neutrality," by Joseph P. Chamberlain, *International Conciliation,* June 1929.

is known that Austria-Hungary also sold similar munitions to the same purchaser . . . the principle of neutrality involved was the same . . . . the United States has always depended upon the right and power to purchase arms and ammunition from neutral nations in case of foreign attack. This right, which it claims for itself, it can not deny to others. . . . The general adoption by the nations of the world of the theory that neutral powers ought to prohibit the sale of arms and ammunition to belligerents . . . would result in every nation becoming an armed camp. . . .[4]

As far back as 1898, at the time of the Spanish-American War, Congress had by Joint Resolution empowered the President to prohibit the export of war material under certain circumstances; but this had been done to prevent military supplies from reaching the Spanish forces in the Carribean. The measure remained in effect until superseded in 1912 by a Joint Resolution (instigated by the turmoil in Mexico) permitting the President to prevent the export of "munitions" to countries on the American continent where there was civil strife. This in turn was extended in 1922 to apply to nations where we enjoyed extraterritorial rights, China being the country chiefly in mind. But the Senate debates on the McReynolds bill revealed strong opposition to the idea that the President should have freedom of choice as to when an embargo should be invoked and as to the nations specifically affected.

[4] "Papers Relating to the Foreign Relations of the United States," 1915, Supplement, The World War, pp. 794-796.

It was a Senate bill which was finally passed. Considerable debate occurred both in the upper and the lower house, and talk even was heard among some of the western Senators about a filibuster to prevent the adjournment of Congress unless the Administration gave way on its demand for discretionary powers. The result represented more of a truce between the Senate and the House (which supported the Administration) than a Senate victory. This was shown by the fact that Section 1 providing for an embargo to be applied impartially to all belligerents was adopted for only a six months' period. The battle was left to be fought again at the 1936 session of Congress.

The President's intention not to let this battle go by default was shown in the comments which he made at the time of signing the Act, especially his protest against "the inflexible provisions of Section 1." These, he said, "might drag us into war instead of keeping us out." And he added, evidently with a broader objection in mind, that "it is the policy of the Government by every peaceful means and without entanglements to coöperate with other similarly minded governments to promote peace." He would have saved himself and the country much trouble if he had vetoed the bill instead of accepting it under protest.

*   *   *

The things which states at war usually seek to acquire abroad may be divided roughly into three categories: first, the actual arms and implements used in military action; second, money and credits to buy arms and other supplies; and third, those multifarious raw materials and manufactured goods which under modern conditions nourish the economy of a nation whether it is at peace or war, furnish the sinews of industry whether it is working for the civilian population or the military, clothe and feed civilians and soldiers alike, and transport them either to the factory or the trenches.

The third category used to be divided into contraband and non-contraband. Certain goods generally recognized under international law as contraband, *i.e.* of direct use in military or naval armaments, were liable to capture if found in transit to the enemy from a neutral. Non-contraband goods were exempt from capture. On the border-line were materials called "conditional contraband," goods liable to seizure if destined for the armed forces. About the contraband list there was always dispute, the neutral trading nation endeavoring to restrict it as much as possible, the blockading belligerent attempting to broaden it. New methods of warfare, involving whole civilian populations and not merely their professional armies, led to such an extension of contraband and conditional contraband that finally in the World War hardly any important article of commerce remained on the free lists of the Allied nations. An American Senator once drily asked whether ostrich feathers had been banned yet.

In effect, the term "contraband" had lost much of its meaning. The repeated demands and protests made by the United States to the Allies, based on its alleged right as a neutral to ship to the Central Powers goods which it claimed were non-contraband, remained demands and protests only; the alleged rights remained without recognition from the Allies. They so remain to this day. As many writers have pointed out, in an era when practically everything is contraband the doctrine of the Freedom of the Seas is dead—killed, so far as its application in any major conflict goes, by the action of the Allies in the World War, by our own eventual acquiescence, and by the changed nature of modern warfare itself.

There used formerly to be a fourth category of exports from neutral to belligerent states—men. But mercenaries are no longer hired out by avaricious sovereigns, and many nations have laws punishing or at least regulating the entry of their citizens into foreign armies.

How far would the neutrality legislation passed by Congress and approved by President Roosevelt August 31, 1935, and the various enactments which amended and superseded it, cover the three cate-

gories of exports referred to above? The answer
to this question will help to indicate whether or not
the action of Congress really constituted an effective
regulation of the principal wartime activities of
private American citizens which might involve the
honor, material interests or sentiments of the American people as a whole.

Section 1 of the Neutrality Act of 1935 prohibited the export of "arms, ammunition or implements of war" from the United States to any port
of a belligerent state, "or to any neutral port for
transshipment to or for the use of a belligerent
country." The President was to define the term
"arms, ammunition or implements of war" and was
authorized, but not compelled, to extend the embargo
to other states which might become involved in a
war. Section 2 of the Act provided for a National
Munitions Control Board and required arms manufacturers to register with it and to obtain from it
licenses for all arms exports. Section 3 prevented
the carrying of arms to or for belligerents on American vessels. And Section 6 provided that if the
President found that the maintenance of peace or
the protection of our citizens so required, he could
proclaim that travel by American citizens on belligerent vessels was at their own risk. The other provisions of the Act were of a technical character, relating to the clearance of vessels and the regulation
or prohibition of the use of our ports by belligerent

submarines. The Act was to come into force with the issuance of a Presidential proclamation "upon the outbreak or during the progress of war between two or more foreign states."

The Act evidently gave the President some discretion, both in choosing the moment for bringing it into effect and in enumerating the arms covered by the embargo. Further latitude was contained in the provision which authorized, but did not make mandatory, the extension of the embargo to other states which might become involved in the war as it progressed.

Former treaties signed by the United States had attempted to define arms and implements of war.[5] These furnished precedents which implied that the list must be narrowly drawn, and certainly drawn to exclude foodstuffs and other raw materials. Senator Pittman, speaking as Chairman of the Foreign Relations Committee during the debate on the bill, said specifically that in his opinion the proposed legislation did not apply to foodstuffs or to raw materials such as cotton. The following colloquy took place on the floor of the Senate. Senator Fletcher, of Florida: "Mr. President, may I inquire of the Senator whether the articles mentioned—implements of war, and so forth—include such commodities as

---

[5]Including the 1925 Geneva Arms Traffic Convention, ratified by the Senate on June 6, 1935, during the same session of Congress which passed the Neutrality Act.

wheat, corn, cotton, meat, and other food products?"
Senator Pittman, of Nevada: "In my opinion, they
do not; nor do I believe they do in the opinion of the
committee, for the reason that today the definition
of arms, ammunition, and implements of war is very
generally recognized in international law."

The President at first seemed cautious about
committing himself as to just what meaning was to
be attributed to the words "arms, ammunition and
implements of war." Indeed, the descriptive phrase
used in the statement which he issued on August 31
when signing the Neutrality Act—"arms, etc."—
was taken by some as indicating a wish to reserve
liberty of action on a wider category of war materials than would seem to be covered in the limited
and explicit phraseology of the Act. This, however,
was only guesswork. The official enumeration of
embargoed articles issued on October 5, when we
declared our neutrality in the Ethiopian war, mentioned almost no articles not directly susceptible of
military use alone. The list met with no criticism,
except perhaps from manufacturers of airplanes and
airplane engines who had hoped that models not
specifically designed for combat might escape
inclusion.

Regarding money and credits for belligerents,
the Act was silent. Senator Pittman indicated that
this was partly because of the complexity of the
problems involved, partly because of the existence of

the so-called "Johnson Act" of April 13, 1934, prohibiting loans to governments in default on obligations to the Government of the United States.[6]
Speaking in the Senate on August 24, Senator
Johnson emphasized that the legislation bearing his
name provided "law enough" to cover effectively all
contingencies likely to arise in the course of the impending Italo-Ethiopian crisis.   For this reason
Congress seemed to think it safe to leave the question of a formal embargo on loans to belligerents
for further investigation and action at a subsequent
session.

In order to answer the widespread demand for
some control over the activities of munitions makers,
and to provide for continuing study of the varied
and complex problems involved, the Act also set up
(Section 2) a permanent National Munitions Control Board, consisting of the Secretaries of State,
the Treasury, War, the Navy and Commerce.   All
manufacturers, exporters and importers of arms,
ammunition and implements of war are required to
register with the Board, which is required to pub-
lish each year the pertinent data which it collects
regarding American individuals and firms engaged
in the munitions industry and trade.   The inclusion
of this provision in the Neutrality Act was largely
fortuitous, due to the public interest aroused by the
hearings of the Nye Committee.   It came into effect

[6]For text see Appendix 3.

November 29, 1935, at which time the State Department announced that 86 firms had so far registered with the Board; warning was given that any manufacturers and distributors which did not register after a short period of grace would be prosecuted.

As already noted, the House of Representatives at that time was in favor of giving the President a broader authority and was against a mandatory arms embargo. It concurred in the Senate bill with some reluctance, and with the proviso that the arms embargo provision should remain in effect for a trial period of only six months.

Consequently, when Congress reconvened in January 1936 it had immediately to reconsider the neutrality question, in view of the fact that the arms embargo provision was coming to an end on February 29. The Ethiopian war was still in progress, but the ineffectiveness of the League's action had somewhat dampened the hopes of those who believed in collective security and correspondingly strengthened the hands of the Senators who desired a rigid law. On February 28, then, a Joint Resolution was passed which deprived the Executive of certain of the discretionary powers which he had been given under the 1935 Act. Under the new terms, the President was to issue his proclamation bringing the embargo into effect whenever he "shall find that there exists a state of war" and not "upon the outbreak or during the progress" of a war.

The law was also amended so that the provisions should be immediately extended to any new belligerents who entered the conflict. Further, Congress added a provision making it unlawful to purchase, sell or exchange bonds of any belligerent government, or political subdivision thereof, or person acting therefor, if issued after the date of the neutrality proclamation. The President was permitted to make exceptions in the case of ordinary commercial credits or short-time obligations in aid of legal transactions and of a character customarily used in normal peacetime commercial transactions. Exceptions were also allowed for renewals or adjustments of such indebtedness. In another field, the amended law provided that it should not apply to an American republic engaged in war against a non-American state unless the republic were coöperating in the war with a non-American state.

Despite the extended debate on the arms embargo provisions, Congress still was not satisfied that it had reached the proper solution. It still was unwilling for its handiwork to be put on the statute books as a permanent part of our neutrality policy. So many members of Congress were disturbed by the trend of the legislation that its passage could not be assured without inclusion of a provision that the arms embargo and certain other sections of the Act dependent thereon should terminate in fourteen months, namely, on May 1, 1937.

2. The Spanish Arms Embargo Resolution of
January 8, 1937

In July 1936 a military rebellion began in Spain. The Neutrality Act of 1935, as amended, related only to international wars, and neither forced nor authorized the Administration to invoke its terms in a civil war. At first there seemed a possibility that certain of the European Powers might succeed in isolating the war in Spain through the Non-Intervention Agreement, which was first proposed on July 26 and regarding which France issued official invitations on August 8.[7] On August 7, Acting Secretary of State Phillips sent a note of instructions to the American diplomatic and consular representative in Spain setting forth what "this Government's position thus far has been and will continue to be." He said: "It is clear that our Neutrality Law with respect to embargo of arms, amunition and implements of war has no application in the present situation since that applies only in the event of war *between and among nations*. On the other hand, in conformity with its well-established policy of non-interference with internal affairs in other countries either in time of peace or in the event of civil strife,

[7] The first formal declarations accepting the agreement regarding non-intervention in Spain were those of Britain and France, both issued August 15. The German, Italian and Soviet Russian declarations were dated August 17, 21 and 23, respectively. The representatives of the accepting Powers did not meet to discuss the plan in detail until September 9.

this Government will, of course, scrupulously refrain from any interference whatsoever in the unfortunate Spanish situation. We believe that American citizens, both at home and abroad, are patri-
otically observing this well-recognized American
policy."[8]

This statement was interpreted as an official inti-
mation that Americans would be unpatriotic to sell
arms even to the legally constituted Spanish Government with which we were on amicable terms. The
announcement of Mr. Phillips' action was made in
Washington on August 11, and, ironically enough,
appeared in the issue of the *New York Times* the
next morning alongside a heading which read: "32
German, Italian Planes Reach Rebel Army in
Spain." Despite the fact that a non-intervention
system had not yet been formally accepted by the
European Powers, the State Department began almost at once (August 22), in written communications to American exporters, to urge them ("moral
suasion") not to sell arms either to the Spanish Government or to the rebels. In this action the American
people probably concurred, though without fully understanding the problems involved or that the State
Department's action, however well-meaning, consti-

---

[8]Department of State Press Release, August 11, 1936. See also
"The Spanish Rebellion and International Law," by Philip C. Jessup,
Foreign Affairs, January 1937.

tuted a departure both from international law and from traditional American practice. Our practice, in fact, in our dealings with certain other countries in this hemisphere, has often been to facilitate the shipment of arms to the recognized government and deny them to their antagonists.

A chief difficulty throughout the American attempt to deal with the neutrality problem has been the tendency both of the Executive and our legislators to assume that the factual situation of the moment, and their feelings with regard to it, have a continuing and permanent basis. We try to legislate to meet a particular situation today and find ourselves hamstrung in dealing with another situation tomorrow. It was so in the case of the war in Spain. The hope that non-intervention might shorten the conflict was attractive; and the movement to restrict the American sale of arms seemed a logical parallel measure. But in practice the embargo did not have the desired results, for the Non-Intervention Agreement reached by the European states proved mere window-dressing, without effective value; while the parallel American embargo remained fully in force.

The specific incident which directly preceded the imposition of a formal embargo by our Government concerned a certain Mr. Cuse, who in December 1937 obtained temporary notoriety by buying up some more or less obsolete airplane equipment which he proposed selling to the Loyalist Government at what the newspapers reported to be a handsome profit to himself. No law existed to prevent his carrying through the transaction or to authorize the Munitions Control Board not to issue licenses to other prospective exporters of arms. Our public always is outraged at the idea of anyone's profiting out of human misery, and when so outraged it often demands action without full deliberation. So it proved in this case. Part of the Cuse shipment of airplanes sailed from New York on the *Mar Cantábrico* on January 7, 1937,[1] attended by much newspaper publicity. Almost overnight a Joint Resolution was rushed through the House and Senate and signed by the President on January 8, 1937, making it unlawful to export arms directly or indirectly to Spain.

The Resolution, which received no negative votes in the Senate and only one in the House, was to remain in effect until the conditions described, namely, a state of civil strife in Spain, should cease to exist.

3. The Neutrality Act of 1937

The passage of the Spanish embargo resolution, quickly regretted in many quarters—including, doubtless, the State Department itself—merely initiated the discussion of neutrality in the Congress which convened in January 1937. The major pro-

[1] The *Mar Cantábrico* was later captured by General Franco's forces before it could reach a Loyalist port.

visions of the 1935 law, extended in February 1936 for fourteen months, were to expire on May 1, 1937. The whole subject was again before Congress.

This time Congress proposed to make a thoroughgoing revision and produce a permanent statute to meet all future exigencies. Members wanted to be rid of the subject. But legislating on neutrality is like digging asphalt out of the bottomless lake in Trinidad. The dent you make quickly disappears. Neutrality has a thousand facets; it presents itself in a new light with each change in the international picture.

By 1937 the world situation had disintegrated to a point where the idea of giving the Executive any power to collaborate in a collective system was more or less abandoned. The Administration no longer expected to obtain a discretionary arms embargo, that is to say, one that would permit discrimination between belligerents; and it even doubted whether it could persuade Congress to give it discretion to fix the moment when the embargo should be applied.

Senator Pittman had introduced into the Senate and Mr. McReynolds into the House drafts of comprehensive neutrality bills which were similar in character, except that as usual the House bill proposed giving the Executive somewhat greater discretion. In the hearings on the Senate bill the State Department spokesman, Assistant Secretary

Moore, gave it a somewhat reluctant and qualified blessing. He clearly indicated that he preferred a third measure, sponsored by Senator Thomas, as being more "flexible." But he went on to say that "being a practical man, and my understanding being that in all human probability the Congress is going to retain that mandatory provision, I say the Pittman Joint Resolution would, as I understand it, be fairly satisfactory."[7]

Just before the expiration of the 1935 Act, Congress adopted the Neutrality Act of 1937—the law now on our statute books.[8] The new Act, signed by the President on May 31, retained with minor changes the mandatory arms embargo, but permitted the President to extend the embargo to civil wars where export of arms "would threaten or endanger the peace of the United States." Thus the idea of the Spanish embargo was taken over, but some discretion was left to the President as to when the embargo should be applied. The civil war must be one which implied a threat to our own peace. The Act also continued the ban on public loans to belligerents, and retained the Munitions Control Board. Travel by Americans on belligerent vessels became unlawful instead of being merely at the risk of the traveller.

[7]*New York Times,* February 24, 1937.
[8]For text see Appendix 5.

The important new feature of the 1937 Act was "cash and carry," sometimes also referred to as "come-and-get-it neutrality." The idea is generally attributed to Mr. Bernard Baruch. Stripped of technicalities, it meant that goods and materials (other than arms, which were embargoed by an earlier provision of the Act) could not be shipped to or for belligerents in American vessels. The President could also provide that all right, title or interest in such shipments must pass to the purchaser before they left the United States; and no insurance on such articles should be deemed to be an American interest. The time of invoking the cash and carry feature of the Act was left to the discretion of the President: it was to come into effect only when he issued a proclamation that a state of war existed and in addition found that the cash and carry provision was "necessary to promote the security or preserve the peace of the United States." The President could also make exceptions as to trade with contiguous states, *i.e.,* Canada and Mexico.

Cash and carry was novel and was enacted for only two years. The 1939 Congress failed to extend it, and no such provision is any longer a part of the law.

* * *

We have now reached the end of our account of legislative enactments on neutrality. But this does not mean that discussion of the subject ceased in Congress with the passage of the 1937 Act. Quite the contrary.

Even before the regular 1939 session of Congress assembled, the Administration realized that there was grave danger of war in Europe in the near future. Our diplomats in foreign capitals seem to have sized up the situation correctly and informed the State Department accurately—in sharp contrast to the absence of warning received from our envoys on the eve of the World War of 1914. In the light of the news from Europe, the Administration determined if possible to get rid of the mandatory arms embargo, which it obviously felt would work in a manner conforming neither with preponderant American sympathies nor with its own view of our national interests. Bills therefore were introduced into the Senate and House which would once again have changed our position drastically. The trade in arms was to be put on a cash and carry basis, like the trade in other goods, and the President was to be allowed to designate danger zones abroad into which American citizens and American ships should not go. The idea was both to tighten up the precautions against untoward incidents due to submarine or airplane warfare and at the same time to avoid banning the purchase of arms by the Western European powers. England and France, who controlled the seas, were ordering airplanes in large numbers from

the United States in a desperate effort to cut down
Germany's long aviation lead. Many persons thought
that the maintenance of the absolute arms embargo,
which meant that in case war came the delivery of
these airplanes and other instruments of war must
cease, might be an encouragement to Germany. They
urged repeal of the embargo as a step to make war
less likely. Isolationist circles pooh-poohed both this
argument and the view that war in Europe was
likely.

The story of the refusal of Congress to strike the
arms embargo from the 1937 Act is too recent history to require elaboration here. It was due to several
causes. Many in Congress were inclined to think that
our foreign diplomats were alarmists and that there
was no need to take action before 1940, when Congress would meet in the regular course of events.
Thus, during a final White House conference at
which President Roosevelt tried to impress some isolationist Senators with the gravity of the situation,
Senator Borah is reported to have challenged the
authenticity and candor of the Administration's
"confidential reports" from Europe, and to have remarked that he felt he possessed just as good information on Europe as Secretary Hull did.[9] In Borah's
opinion there was not going to be any war anyhow.
While Senator Nye, who fought amendment of the

[9] *New York Times,* July 20, 1939.

Act as vigorously as he had worked for amendment of the Spanish Embargo Resolution a short time before, issued a statement just after the conclusion of the Senate fight in which he went so far as to give his opinion that the President, for some unspecified and therefore presumably sinister reason, "looks upon another foreign war at this time as somewhat desirable"—a statement as wide of the mark as his prophecy that war was not coming.

The Administration probably made a mistake in not pressing the issue until late in the Congressional session when mental and physical fag had taken their toll and the days were hot. Unfortunately, and perhaps unnecessarily, the issue took on a partisan aspect. Defeat of the plan for revision became linked with the desire of the President's opponents to weaken his personal prestige in other fields. The final vote by which the Senate Committee refused to report out the bill (12 to 11) was a vote "against Roosevelt" even more than a vote against raising the arms embargo.

Such is the history of our neutrality legislation over the past four years. It was against this background that President Roosevelt called Congress to meet again on September 21, 1939, to discuss once more the question of revision. With Europe in the throes of a desperate struggle, the decisions to be taken in Washington were obviously of critical importance, both materially and psychologically—for the participants, and for those European nations still clinging to neutrality. They would also affect our own ability to remain out of the conflict, though precisely how was a matter of serious dispute.

CHAPTER VI

THE EXPERIENCE OF THREE WARS

FROM the foregoing summary of our 1935-1937 neutrality legislation we see that the three wars of this period all played a part in shaping American thought and policy. Each part was different. The imminence of the first of these wars hastened the adoption of the 1935 Act and colored its content. The second war, that in Spain, was responsible for special *ad hoc* action by Congress and the Executive; and the failure of the embargo to achieve its objectives was disconcerting to many sections of American opinion. The third war, though it did not require Washington to call any neutrality statute into play, nevertheless had its effect on American opinion also. Indeed, we may say that the degree to which the Spanish Embargo Resolution proved unsatisfactory in practice, and the realization of how narrowly the United States had escaped having to apply the 1937 Act in a manner that would have harmed China and helped Japan, began opening some American eyes to the limitations and risks of the legislative course upon which Congress had somewhat optimistically embarked.

The War in Ethiopia

When early in October 1935 the Italo-Ethiopian war at last became an incontrovertible fact, President Roosevelt issued two proclamations, both dated October 5,[1] to give effect to the wishes of Congress as set forth in the Neutrality Act. One declared that a state of war existed, admonished the public to observe the provisions of the Act, and enumerated the articles considered arms, ammunition and implements of war. The other (released a day later, on October 6) warned American citizens to abstain from traveling on any vessels of either of the belligerent nations, and added: "I do hereby give notice that any citizen . . . who may travel on such a vessel, contrary to the provisions of the said Joint Resolution, will do so at his own risk."

The President hastened to make plain that he did not think his duty stopped with invoking the letter of the law. Simultaneously with publishing the first of the above proclamations he issued a statement through the State Department which, after referring to "the situation which has unhappily developed between Ethiopia and Italy," concluded with the follow-

[1]There had been on this date no formal declaration of war; in fact there never was one. At this time, though Italian troops had crossed the frontier between Eritrea and Ethiopia, there had been no rupture of diplomatic relations. Speaking some weeks later, on Armistice Day, President Roosevelt referred to his prompt proclamation that hostilities had begun. He said: "We are acting to simplify definitions and facts by calling war 'war' when armed invasion and a resulting killing of human beings take place."

ing warning: "In these specific circumstances I desire it to be understood that any of our people who voluntarily engage in transactions of any character with either of the belligerents do so at their own risk."

Some observers who knew what a break this announcement made with the past have said that the American public did not comprehend the momentous decision which lay hidden in that one sentence. Probably this was true. The Freedom of the Seas, if in modern times it ever existed, had received another blow, and this time from its staunchest friend; American trade with nations at war was no longer (at any rate pending some reversal of policy) to enjoy the protection of the American Government; and this loss of what Jefferson had called "inalienable rights," what Wilson had called "acknowledged rights," had been accepted by the public almost unnoticed and almost without complaint.

The reason was twofold. To whatever extent the public did realize the magnitude of the American sacrifice of rights formerly prized, it probably thought that in the abstract the renunciation was wise. For it remembered that the policy which the Administration was now reversing was the policy which had involved the United States in both of the great wars fought in Europe since the achievement of American independence—the Napoleonic Wars and the World War. Above all, for the moment the step cost nothing; there was little or no trade with Ethiopia, and the trade with Italy continued unaffected.[2] It is a question whether the public would have remained so indifferent if (taking a situation like that in 1914 or today, 1939) the warships of some Power had begun seizing or sinking American shipments of cotton and wheat and copper and oil, and if to the protests of our shippers, and of the farmers and miners and factory workers lined up behind them, our Government simply said: "You took the risk. We will not help you."

The Executive admonition of October 5 was to be repeated and amplified during October and November. On October 10, Secretary Hull said:

The warning given by the President in his proclamation concerning travel on belligerent ships and his general warning that during the war any of our people who voluntarily engage in transactions of any character with either of the belligerents do so at their own risk were based upon the policy and purpose of keeping this country out of war—keeping it from being drawn into war. It certainly was not intended to encourage transactions with the belligerents.[3]

State Department officials assured newspaper men that this was not designed to support the program of sanctions against Italy then under consid-

[2]According to the New York Times of October 9, business executives questioned at a meeting of the Export Managers Club of New York the day previous revealed that they were not going to be deterred by the President's warning that trade would be at their own risk.

[3]Department of State Press Releases, October 12, 1935.

eration by the League of Nations. They did not deny, however, that it might be considered as a retort to the objections telegraphed to President Roosevelt on October 7 by a group of indignant New York exporters who saw in the Administration's warning a threat to a possibly lucrative trade in war materials, and even to the continuance of their normal peacetime trade with Italy.

On October 7, the same day that news of the President's first proclamation became known in Geneva, and the day Italy announced the fall of Adowa, the League Council accepted the report of its "Committee of Six" which pronounced the following unprecedented verdict: "The Italian Government has resorted to war in disregard of its covenants under Article XII of the Covenant of the League of Nations." On October 10 the Assembly of the League ratified the verdict. On October 11 the "Committee of Coördination" of the Assembly moved to apply sanctions by imposing an arms embargo against Italy, utilizing for the purpose the same list of arms, ammunition and implements of war which President Roosevelt had used; and simultaneously League states which had prohibited or restricted the export of arms to Ethiopia agreed to annul such measures.[4] On October 14 the same Committee proposed to cut off loans and credits to Italy. By October 19 agreement was reached on a

[4]President Roosevelt under the terms of the Neutrality Act had no power to discriminate between the belligerents.

broad boycott of Italian exports, on an embargo on the shipment to Italy of a number of key war materials, and on other measures aimed at bringing Italy to an observance of the promises it had made in the League Covenant (and incidentally in the Briand-Kellogg Pact).

In the United States, meanwhile, another development was beginning also to attract attention. On October 8 a news item from Washington noted that for about two months the Italian port of Massaua, in Eritrea, had been the chief importing point in the world for American motor trucks. The appearance of this item happened to synchronize with publication of several accounts from American correspondents in Eritrea detailing the achievements of Italian road building and describing the progress of the Italian Army via truck. A few days later (October 19) the Commerce Department disclosed that the United States had been supplying a part of Italy's increased foreign purchases of many products used in making munitions, including cotton waste, iron and steel scrap, copper, benzol, and various chemicals.[5]

These various developments presented the American Government with two alternatives: (1) The Administration could wait until Geneva actually set in operation a system of sanctions, which obviously was bound to include an embargo by the League

[5]*New York Times,* October 20, 1935.

Powers on many goods which were also being shipped from the United States to Italy. In that event, and if the League tried to reinforce sanctions with a blockade, the American Government would have either to bow to League pressure or to condone exploitation by American traders of the efforts being made by European nations to preserve peace and live up to their treaty obligations. There would be the added risk in the offing, moreover, that American commercial interests might become so enamored of a lucrative war trade that they would demand diplomatic protection and (strengthened by the fact of American unemployment) might eventually involve us in dangerous disputes with the members of the League. Or (2), the Administration might presume that the American people's interest in peace was so intense that it would support any move calculated to prevent the United States from being put in the uncomfortable position of thwarting Europe's collective action for peace, and which at the same time promised to diminish the risk of its own involvement.

The President's statement of October 5 showed that from the start he inclined toward the second course. His feeling apparently became stronger as the League program took shape, though it was repeatedly stated very explicitly on his behalf that he was not actuated by any feeling of obligation toward the League or under the influence of any pledge or

any understanding of any description with Great
Britain or any other Power.   Doubtless he was encouraged by the fact that several western Senators,
among them as redoubtable an isolationist as Senator Borah, seemed tacitly to approve what he was
trying to do.   They protested that there must not
be coördination of policy between the United States
and the League.   On the other hand, they did not
seem ready to let their inveterate mistrust of the
League carry them quite to the point of risking a
fight with all the League Powers in order to trade
with an aggressor designated at Geneva.   They did
not reveal whether or not they would approve if the
Administration chose not to consider the members
of the League as belligerents in case Geneva's effort
to curb Italy led to hostilities.   But for the time
being no decision on that point was necessary.

On November 28 Senator Borah elaborated his
views in a prepared statement.   He said that he
understood that the Government was acting "wholly
apart from the League," but he said he thought it
"very reasonable" for us to seek "to hold our exports down to a normal peace basis" as a means
of "manifesting our purpose not to take advantage
of the war to make war profits."   In giving out
the statement, he remarked: "I want to help the
Government pursue its general course."[6]

[6]*New York Times,* November 29, 1935.

A parallel appeal never again to countenance war profits was made by Senator Bennett Champ Clark, Democrat, of Missouri, in the December issue of *Harpers*. Calling the 1935 Neutrality Act a "stop gap," he said that food, clothing, lumber, leather and chemicals are all as important aids in winning a war as are munitions, and made plain that he would favor new legislation restricting the export of all of them. Perhaps sensing that there were some practical limits—politically as well as economically— to the course he proposed, he avoided specific mention of "cotton" or "copper," though they certainly are among the raw materials most useful to a belligerent.

Senator Vandenberg in a radio talk on December 19 called for a neutrality program "unrelated to the League of Nations." The American people must, he said, "make no loans; grant no credits; ship no arms, ammunition or implements of war to *any* belligerent." "We should prohibit American travel on belligerent ships," he said. And he added: "In the field of general commodities the prospect is less clear. But a quota system, confining commerce to a peace-time rate, or a 'cash and carry' system, making deliveries at our own seaboard, may well offer a basis for solution." Finally, he said "we must make our neutrality legislation mandatory."[7]

But already in October, long before the last of these statements had appeared, the Administration

[7]Press release of the Columbia Broadcasting System.

had thought it necessary to intensify its effort to prevent American traders from seeking what was frequently referred to in the Washington dispatches as "blood money." Passing beyond the original warning that American traders could not expect to receive government support if they got into trouble over shipments of goods to warring nations, the State Department adopted the position that such trade should definitely be discouraged and restricted.

On October 30 (three days before the League fixed on November 18 as the date for starting sanctions against Italy, but when Geneva dispatches already indicated that a date was about to be set), the President issued a statement in which he made clear that he favored restricting exports to belligerents to the average of such sales in normal times. He said in part:

This Government is determined not to become involved in the controversy and is anxious for the restoration and maintenance of peace.

However, in the course of war, tempting trade opportunities may be offered to our people to supply materials which would prolong the war. I do not believe that the American people will wish for abnormally increased profits that temporarily might be secured by greatly extending our trade in such materials; nor would they wish the struggles on the battlefield to be prolonged because of profits accruing to a comparatively small number of American citizens.

Accordingly, the American Government is keeping informed as to all shipments consigned for export to both belligerents.

Simultaneously Secretary Hull said that he wished to

reiterate and call special attention to the definite implications and the effect of the policy of this Government to discourage dealings with the two belligerent nations as set forth in the President's public statement of October 5 and my statement of October 10 warning our people not to trade with the belligerents except at their own risk.

And he added a strong argument that "an early peace, with the restoration of normal business and normal business profits, is far sounder and far preferable to temporary and risky war profits." [8]

The statements by the President and Secretary of State were in the nature of a threat. How it might be carried out was not revealed. But the public before long was given the detailed information which evidently had provoked the President and Secretary of State into taking so decided a stand. On November 5 the Department of Commerce announced that American shipments of oil to Italy had been 600 percent larger in August and September 1935 than in the same two months the year previous. Further, when the export figures for October came to hand[9] they showed important increases in the amounts sent to Italy of what might be called "war sinews," though total exports to Italy had increased in value only from $6,184,491 in October 1934 to

[8]Department of State Press Releases, November 2, 1935.

[9]Department of Commerce news release, November 23, 1935.

$6,821,366 in October 1935, as that country was cutting down on materials not useful in war in order to conserve exchange.

Evidently worried by the growing trade in war materials, Secretary Hull on November 15 referred with emphatic disapproval to the shipment of what he termed "essential war materials." He mentioned by name oil, copper, trucks, tractors, scrap iron and scrap steel. "This class of trade," he said, "although not actually 'arms, ammunition or implements of war,' is directly contrary to the policy of this Government as announced in official statements of the President and the Secretary of State, as it is also contrary to the general spirit of the recent Neutrality Act." He added that the Administration was "closely observing the trend and volume of exports" to the two belligerent countries. In the effort to reinforce moral suasion, the Department of Commerce on November 23 sent out letters to American shipping concerns calling the attention of owners and operators of ships under mortgage to the Government that "the carrying of essential war materials such as those mentioned in the statement of the Secretary of State, November 15, destined for either of the belligerents is distinctly contrary to the policy of the Government." It was estimated that the Government had about $97,000,000 outstanding in ship construction loans, and a large amount more due on vessels purchased by various companies.

It was about at this point that some concern began to be felt in Washington lest in its determination not to interfere with or be entangled in a League system of sanctions the Administration might have gone further than necessitated by any actual developments in Europe. The proposal to widen the embargo on raw materials for Italy had gained backing at Geneva, and it was reported that oil, coal, copper and steel might all be added to the list. On November 30 the "Committee of Eighteen" was called for December 12 to consider extending the sanctions against Italy to include oil. Geneva dispatches mentioned that in the discussion of all these proposals the Hull list of November 15 figured prominently. The State Department professed not to be worried by this fact. The declaration was repeatedly made that the neutrality policy of the Administration had been adopted to keep the country out of involvement in the African war, that no pressure from those greedy for war profits would swerve it from its goal, and that it would follow the course it had chosen regardless of what other countries or the League of Nations might do.

The November figures for American exports to the warring nations[10] further substantiated the Washington statement that in certain respects our trade was profiting from the war in Africa although the profit consisted largely in the shift of our exports

[10]Department of Commerce news release, December 21, 1935.

to materials useful in war as the total had increased
little. In November 1934 total exports to Italy were
valued at $8,418,608; in November 1935 the value
was $9,054,915. Non-metallic minerals (including
oil) increased from $497,565 to $1,304,722. Metals
and manufactures (except machinery and vehicles)
rose from $872,071 to $2,026,622. Machinery and
vehicles rose from $466,331 to $1,187,383. These
were the chief increases. Exports of cotton fell.
The total exports to Italian Africa rose from $17,971
in October 1934 to $583,735 in October 1935. Ex-
ports to Ethiopia remained negligible.

Meanwhile in Europe there seemed to come a
realization that the Neutrality Act as passed by
Congress, though a welcome aid to the League in
trying to deal with the war in Ethiopia, might turn
out to be a two-edged sword. As Harold Callender
cabled prophetically to the *New York Times* from
London on December 4:

> It cuts away the once formidable obstacle to a collective
> blockade, the freedom of the seas policy of the United States.
> It hits Italy harder than Ethiopia and so reinforces League
> sanctions. But in a future war it might penalize the nations
> applying sanctions instead of penalizing the aggressor, and
> its adverse effect might be most keenly felt by the nation
> best able to control the seas—that is, Britain.

As to the President's elaboration of the policy
laid down by Congress, namely the attempt to discourage all "abnormal" trade with a belligerent,

there apparently was still more apprehension, especially in London. Even then farsighted observers were realizing that the arguments which the Administration had been using might commend themselves so strongly to the American public that Congress at its next session would translate the policy into mandatory law, with the result that in a war between Great Britain and Germany the United States would be unable to provision the British Isles even though its sympathies might be strongly with a democracy and against a dictatorship, and even though the British fleet was in command of the seas. As Mr. Callender pointed out, whether a nation was fighting in self-defense or for conquest, it would be deprived of access to American supplies. The same fear found expression in the United States from other observers who emphasized the unwisdom of changing the rules of our neutrality just before some war breaks out or after it has actually begun, and suggested that we could not have one neutrality policy to apply to Italy in the Ethiopian war and a different policy in, say, a war between Italy and Britain or between Germany and the League Powers.[11]

It was certainly correct to stress that our neutrality policy should be broadly considered and not directed mainly to the very peculiar circumstances of the Italian war in Africa, or, indeed to

[11]Walter Lippmann in the *New York Herald Tribune*, December 5 and 7, 1935.

any specific war. On the other hand, what we think
chiefly desirable is that any neutrality law should
be sufficiently flexible so that we can forego certain
privileges of trade if we think such action is wisest
in the particular circumstances, without being too
much worried about the precedent which thereby
might be created for a different set of circumstances
when we might decide that it was impracticable or
unnecessary to renounce our trade to the same extent. The mere fact that we have decided not to
exercise a right in one situation is not necessarily
conclusive as to our action in the future. When we
pass neutrality legislation we are not primarily interested in making a contribution to international
law. Indeed, we do not so much make law as provide
a vehicle for making policy—the policy best suited to
keeping us out of trouble.

The Ethiopian war ended, for all practical purposes, with the flight of Emperor Haile Selassie on
May 2, 1936. President Roosevelt removed the embargo on the export of arms to Italy and Ethiopia
on June 20. The League of Nations recommended
the lifting of sanctions against Italy on July 4.

The War in Spain

We have described in a previous chapter how
Washington reacted to the outbreak of General
Franco's rebellion in Spain in the summer of 1936,

and how in January 1937 Congress passed, and
President Roosevelt signed, an embargo resolution
prohibiting the export of arms to either side. In
the early stages of the war, be it repeated, the
American Government hoped that the Non-Intervention Agreement would work (though this
hardly explains the State Department's hurry to
make American citizens realize their "patriotic"
duty not to sell arms to the legal Spanish Government, an abrupt departure from our traditional
practice).

But the Non-Intervention Agreement did not
work. At the present time there is no further doubt
on this point. By the admission of Rome and Berlin, it is now established that from the very first days
of the war and up to the very end the Italian and
German Governments sent airplanes, artillery and
munitions of all sorts to aid General Franco, and
that while the German contribution in men was in
the form mainly of aviators and technicians, the
Italian Army contributed members of its organized
units to a total admitted to be 40,000 men and estimated variously by foreign military experts all the
way from that figure up to 100,000. It is part of
the tactics of totalitarian régimes, well expounded in
"Mein Kampf," to assume that a lie will be believed
if it is big enough and to consider international
agreements mere tactical manœuvres. In accordance
with this strategy, Italy and Germany always denied

that they were helping General Franco. It was less surprising to those familiar with "Mein Kampf" than to other persons to read in dispatches from Rome and Berlin in the spring of 1939, after the Spanish war was over, boastful accounts of the numbers of Italian and German troops who had fought in Spain, the number of tons of bombs dropped by Italian and German army aviators from Italian and German army planes on Spanish cities, and the decisive nature of this intervention in winning the war for Franco. Needless to say, all this action was contrary to the terms of the Non-Intervention Agreement to which Italy and Germany had adhered, and to their official statements at the time.

Nor, on the other hand, has any secret been made by representatives of the Spanish Loyalist Government of the fact that after the Franco rebellion began they looked in any and all directions for help in suppressing it. For a moment, following the disclosure of Italian military help to Franco when Italian airplanes crashed in French Morocco en route from Italy to Spanish Morocco, the Spanish Government hoped that the French Government with which it was on friendly terms would continue to permit it to secure arms in accordance with international law and usage. But London urged Paris to refrain, and went so far as to tell the French Government that if it were tempted into selling arms to the Loyalists, and if France as a result became involved in a European war, she need expect no help from across the Channel. French policy varied. At moments when Italian and German help became particularly obvious, or when "mystery" submarines began raiding shipping engaged in trade with Loyalist Spain, the French Government would open the Pyrenees frontier to shipments of supplies from other European countries. The chief provider of arms to Loyalist Spain was Soviet Russia. The first Russian shipment of arms reached Spain about October 20—almost three months after the Italian army planes crashed in French North Africa. Ex-Premier Negrin and others have admitted the Russian shipments, saying merely that when the Government's natural sources of supply failed they bought arms from anyone—even, indirectly, from Germany. Americans may find this an unexpected result of embargoing American shipments of arms.

The whole Spanish experience seems to us to prove that an embargo has no utility as a general peace measure unless it is imposed not only by the United States but by the other important munition-producing countries, and that even so it should not be adopted without some mechanism for repeal in case the other participants in the restrictive action do not abide by their word.

We shall not pause here to appraise the causes of the Spanish war, or to show how rival ideologies became connected in the American mind with the

two contestants. Partisans of each side became
extremely vocal in the United States. Large sums
of money were raised for relief, particularly by
Loyalist supporters. Several thousand Americans
volunteered to fight on the Loyalist side "against
Italy and Germany." There also developed a strong
movement to repeal the embargo. Even Senator
Nye had become restive when he saw how the embargo was actually working out in practice, and he
introduced in the Senate a bill which would have
raised the embargo solely as regards the Spanish
Loyalists. It is interesting that such a proposal
should have emanated from a man who has opposed
any flexibility whatever in legislation in this field
and who presumably will usually be found among
the most vigorous opponents of changes in any
general neutrality act during the progress of a war.
In any event, the Nye bill was opposed by Secretary Hull, who wrote to Chairman Pittman of the
Foreign Relations Committee as follows :[12]

In the form in which it is presented, the proposed legislation, if enacted, would shift the embargo, which is now being
applied against both parties to the conflict in Spain, in
respect of shipments of arms to one party while leaving in
effect the embargo in respect to shipments to the other party.
Even if the legislation applied to both parties, its enactment
would still subject us to unnecessary risks we have so far
avoided. We do not know what lies ahead in the Spanish
situation. The original danger still exists. In view of the

[12]See Department of State Press Releases, May 13, 1938.

continued danger of international conflict arising from the
circumstances of the struggle, any proposal which at this
juncture contemplates a reversal of our policy of strict non-
intervention which we have thus far so scrupulously followed, and under the operation of which we have kept out
of involvements, would offer a real possibility of complications.

For some time there had been insistent demands
in many quarters that the Executive branch of the
Government should not await legislation to raise
the embargo. To these the State Department replied that it had no authority to take any such
action so long as there prevailed in Spain a state of
civil strife similar to that which had existed when
the Spanish Arms Embargo Resolution and the 1937
Neutrality Act were adopted and applied to the
Spanish situation.[13]

The opposite view was expressed in some detail
by ex-Secretary of State Stimson in a statement to
the *New York Times*.[14] Basing his opinion on what
he called "simple and long-standing principles of
American interests and conduct," he asserted that
the change in international situation during the past
two years would justify the raising of the embargo
by the Executive. He wrote:

The embargo, which by the terms of the law authorizing it
was intended as a protection against conditions which would

[13]See letter from Secretary Hull to Raymond Leslie Buell. Department of State Press Releases, March 22, 1938.

[14]*New York Times,* January 24, 1939.

endanger the peace of the United States, is now shown by the events of the past two years to be itself a source of danger to that peace. Any danger that may come to the people of the United States from the situation in Spain would arise not from any lawful sale of munitions in our markets to the Government of Spain, but from the assistance which our embargo has given to the enemies of Spain.[15]

We need not pursue the subject. The Spanish arms embargo expired with the ending of the Spanish war. It is sufficient for our present purpose to point out that neither as a measure to ensure domestic tranquillity nor as a measure to shorten the Spanish war did the arms embargo have the desired effect. Those charged with its application must have become heartily sick when they saw it become an instrument in the hands of the German and Italian totalitarian governments for extending their influence in Spain.

The War in China

It seems somewhat anomalous to discuss the operation of a law in a situation where in fact it was never applied. In the Sino-Japanese war, which in effect started in September 1931 and became a general conflict of great proportions by 1937, neither the United States nor any other Great Power declared its neutrality.

[15]For a reply by Martin Conboy, and a rebuttal of Mr. Conboy by Charles C. Burlingham and Philip C. Jessup, see the *New York Times*, January 26 and 31, 1939.

Our neutrality statutes at that time provided that "whenever the President shall find that there exists a state of war" he shall make a proclamation under the Neutrality Act. He did not find in 1937 that there existed a state of war in China, nor has he done so since; and his failure to invoke the Neutrality Act has had the general support of Congress and of the people.

Neither Japan nor China formally declared war. Probably no technicality of this sort was intended to act as a deterrent when the 1935 Act was passed. In fact, in the hearings on one of the earlier neutrality bills, Judge Walton Moore, Assistant Secretary of State, was quite categorical in his assurance that when a war "actually occurred" there rested upon the President a duty to make a proclamation and to do so without delay.[16] But neither Judge Moore nor anyone else could foretell that there would be a war in China in which our declaration of neutrality would appear to be directly contrary to our national interests and certainly contrary to the overwhelming sentiment of the American people.

Senator Pittman took account of a prevalent American feeling when, in explaining the failure to apply the Act in the China war, he said that Japan was disseminating a war "disease" which might in-

[16]Statement of R. Walton Moore, Assistant Secretary of State, before Committee on Foreign Affairs, House of Representatives, January 7, 1936.

volve the rest of the world. He recommended that
Japan should be quarantined "as every civilized
community quarantines against contagious disease."
The Neutrality Act, he said, "never was intended to
meet such contagion. It was intended solely to
eliminate certain causes which might lead us into a
foreign war."[17] So, in pungent language, the Senator
who was most largely responsible for the 1937 Act
quite clearly intimates that where the Act does not
meet the purpose for which it was intended, it should
not, despite its terms, be invoked.

To have imposed the arms embargo in the
Chinese situation would not have seriously penalized
Japan. As an industrialized country it is far more
interested in raw materials and scrap iron (which
can freely be exported under the Act) than in the
manufactured product. China, on the other hand,
needed airplanes, which it could not fabricate itself,
and arms and other implements of war which only a
great industrial effort could produce. Besides wanting manufactured goods, China was badly in need
of the financial resources to purchase them and at
the same time to acquire vitally essential raw materials such as oil. Had we declared our neutrality
in the Sino-Japanese war, it obviously would have
been wholly unneutral and contrary to every principle of international law for our Government to
aid China financially. In the absence of such a

[17]*New York Herald Tribune,* October 7, 1937.

declaration, however, we could give substantial financial assistance, and did. On December 15, 1938, Jesse Jones, Chairman of the Reconstruction Finance Corporation, announced that the Export-Import Bank had authorized credits in the amount of $25,000,000 to the Universal Trading Corporation of New York, as the Chinese governmental purchasing agency in the United States was high-soundingly called. It was stated that the credit was to finance the export of American agricultural and manufactured products to China and the import of wood oil from China. At about the same time, Great Britain also granted a credit to China.[18] A few days later, on December 19, the Secretary of the Treasury announced that the United States had decided to continue its extension of credit to China against gold accumulated in this country through the sale of silver. Mr. Morgenthau is reported to have denied that this was in violation of "the spirit of the Neutrality Act," saying: "Who's at war? We are simply extending credit to a friendly nation."[19]

In addition to the substantive aid which we extended to China there was the counterpart of discouraging the furnishing of military aid to Japan. On June 11, 1938, Secretary Hull revealed that the State Department had unofficially discouraged the sale of American airplanes to Japan, much as had

[18]*New York Times,* December 16, 1938.
[19]*New York Times,* December 20, 1938.

been done during the Ethiopian war and with regard
to munitions exports to Spain after the outbreak of
the conflict there and before the Arms Embargo
Resolution became effective. The Department tried
to couch its public warnings in terms which might
not directly offend Japan; that country was not
named by Secretary Hull, who merely expressed displeasure at the shipment of airplanes to countries
using aircraft for aërial bombardment of civil populations. But the Department's meaning was quite
clear, and apparently in its dealings with the airplane
manufacturers its representations were more specific.
In any event, the sale of airplanes to Japan by American manufacturers came to a stop. Here again,
moral suasion was effective, but in this case moral
suasion had a real punch. The Government was
far and away the greatest purchaser of aircraft
from private companies. No one of them could risk
incurring the displeasure of the Administration, with
the possible consequence that it would lose essential
orders from our War and Navy Departments.

Another step taken in Washington which possibly bore more heavily on Japan than on China was
the prohibition against the use of government-owned
merchant vessels for the transport to either Japan or
China of any of the arms, munitions or implements of
war which had been listed in the proclamation made
under the 1937 Act. A statement by the President to
this effect on September 14, 1937, further specified

that other merchant vessels flying the American flag could transport such articles to Japan or China at their own risk. For a moment it seemed that we were close to invoking the Neutrality Act in the Chinese war, as the President added: "The question of applying the Neutrality Act remains in *statu quo,* the Government's policy remaining on a twenty-four hour basis."

In the almost continuous discussion of neutrality throughout the whole period of the war in China, even the most hardened critics of the President seemed to find no serious objection to the course he was following—failing to invoke the Neutrality Act, and throwing our influence and to some extent our material force on the side of China. More clearly than any other incident in recent American history, our experience in the Sino-Japanese war shows that what we conceive at the moment to be in the best interest of the nation, rather than any hidebound conception of neutrality, is the guiding factor in determining our action.

CHAPTER VII

DEVICES TO KEEP OUT OF WAR

A NY neutrality legislation enacted in the vacuum of peace cannot be more than a framework which we raise in the hope that it will support the specific policy which later on we will adopt to keep the country out of a specific war. In advance of the crisis, the best we can do is to set up certain simple rules which may help the Government deal prudently with each problem as it arises.

As already indicated, consistency must yield to self-interest and the policy which we adopt today cannot always conform to the past, and need not necessarily do so. The World War precedents are useless, and may even be dangerous. Nor, turning to more recent days, are we likely to find much positive help from our experience in the period of the Ethiopian, the Chinese or the Spanish wars. The one lesson we should have learned from those three wars is that the successive laws which were enacted in that period were for the most part either inapplicable, or proved highly unsatisfactory where applied.

The title of this book—"Can America Stay Neutral?"—implies that it will make some attempt to answer the question. A good part of the answer is contained in the statement that the *legislation* we adopt will not—and certainly *should* not—be decisive. The war upon which the world has just entered may go through many phases; the fortunes of the contestants will vary; new arenas will be opened to combat; new instruments of destruction may be found and new tactics used. Whether or not we remain neutral must depend solely upon the continually developing opinion of the people, Congress and the Executive. Together they should appraise each change as it occurs, in order to determine whether any vital American interest impels us, too, to assume the terrific burden and make the terrific sacrifice of war. As Colonel Lindbergh said on September 15, 1939, "We should never enter a war unless it is absolutely essential to the future welfare of our nation."

The sole purpose of legislation such as we have been discussing is to prevent the country from reaching a decision on the great question of peace or war in the passion aroused by some incidental happening or because material interests have been infringed upon after being unwisely engaged. The treatment which our trade or even our citizens may receive from belligerents, even if lawless, is not in itself an adequate reason for the United States to abandon neutrality unless the attacks are deliberate and direct. If we start by insisting upon technical rights we are likely to follow the same course as in the years preceding 1812 and 1917.[1]

[1]This does not mean that our Government should be expected to make any sweeping renunciation of American rights. That would

Forces of a different character, perhaps political, perhaps moral, may come into play. They may become so overwhelming in their impact that our people will come to feel that vital interests are at stake and that these can be saved only by resort to war. This is not the subject we are treating here. We are discussing the attempt to minimize by legislative means some of the risks of war. In this sphere let us realize plainly that no domestic legislation of a self-denying character can prevent other nations from endangering our vital interests. We cannot legislate ourselves into peace in a world at war.

With this introduction, and in the hope of separating possibly helpful elements of our recent neutrality legislation from possibly dangerous ones, we propose to examine briefly each of its substantive provisions, as well as the various proposals which have recently been made to supplement or alter it.

---

be to invite trouble. It was natural, then, for Secretary Hull, in his statement of September 14, 1939, to affirm that the Government "has not abandoned any of its rights as a neutral under international law." He went on to say that under domestic law our nationals are required to refrain from the exercise of certain of their rights under international law but that this did not imply the abandonment of these "or indeed of any, neutral rights." The Government, he said, would adopt "such measures as may seem practical and prudent when those rights are violated by any of the belligerents." It will be interesting to follow our Government's course of action and to see what rights of international law will be maintained and how they will be maintained. In any representations that become necessary our Government's treatment of the *Panay* incident might well serve as a model. The belligerents, or their nationals, probably possess sufficient property within our jurisdiction to satisfy substantial claims for damages for any wanton acts committed against our nationals. (For text of the Hull statement see Appendix 14.)

1. *The Arms Embargo*

From the very beginning of the neutrality debate —and even earlier—the idea of an arms embargo has been a storm center. Unfortunately it has acquired a prominence which is perhaps exaggerated from the point of view of its material effect on the outcome of a European war or on our ability to remain a neutral. But due to this prominence, and because other issues have been injected into the debate, the psychological effect of our either repealing or maintaining the embargo will be enormous.

Today those who favor the lifting of the embargo are being attacked as interventionists, warmongers and blind supporters of the British and French cause. Those who oppose repeal are called isolationists or even labelled as pro-German. Some quarters say our sons would follow our guns—that the sale of arms, even on a cash and carry basis, would be the first step toward sending our boys to Europe. Others argue that to sell arms to whoever can pay for them and get them is in harmony with our traditional practice, is truly impartial, and that our real danger of being involved in the present war arises not from any risk inherent in selling arms but from the possibility of the war's being prolonged or of its threatening to lead to the victory of a group of Powers with which we could not live satisfactorily and permanently at peace.

The facts of the matter are that throughout our history until 1935 the arms embargo had been no part of American policy. We gained our independence in part as a result of the arms which we received from abroad. Subsequently we insisted upon the right of our citizens to ship arms abroad in all wars where we were a neutral, with the sole exception of certain civil wars in this hemisphere and in the Far East where we permitted shipments only to the legally constituted governmental authorities.

With the passage of time, any legalistic reason for an embargo solely on arms has decreased rather than increased. The distinction between absolute and conditional contraband now has no practical significance. To the extent that it does have any significance, we can say that shipments of arms are less likely to involve us in disputes than shipments of other goods, because the right of a belligerent to seize and confiscate arms destined for the enemy is universally recognized and any incidental loss of American life is not likely to rouse violent feelings in this country.

Plainly, however, a strong sentiment has been built up recently in support of the arms embargo. The public thinks of weapons of destruction as falling into a different category, sentimentally and morally, from any other sort of materials which might be purchased by foreign belligerents. Somehow, we all look back on 1917 wheat at $3.25 a bushel and wartime cotton at 38 cents a pound with less distaste than we recall the 200 percent stock dividend of the Bethlehem Steel Corporation in January 1917 and the wartime profits of munition makers. But in plain fact there is no very strong practical reason for making this differentiation. Food and clothing are as necessary to an army as guns; scrap iron feeds the maw of Mars as efficiently as the airplane engine propels him to his chosen field of destruction.

To rule out all arms shipments by all neutrals to all belligerents in every war would merely force every country to become an armed camp in anticipation of possible hostilities. Each country would have to rely solely upon its own ability to create the arms needed for its defense. Weak countries, or agricultural countries which have no munitions industries, would always be at the mercy of stronger or more industrialized neighbors. For example, as already noted, if impartial arms embargoes had customarily been imposed upon all belligerents at the time of our Revolutionary War, the effect on the fortunes of our struggling young republic might have been disastrous. If the arms embargo is to become a permanent part of our policy, other countries which would normally buy from us must either

become self-sufficient in arms or make prompt plans
to find some other source of supply. Otherwise they
risk being cut off at the exact moment when their
need for arms becomes most acute. Do we wish to
see each of the South American countries attempt
to establish its own munitions industry, or, in the
alternative, turn to European manufacturers?
Further, if the present European conflict is prolonged and the arms embargo remains on the statute
books, we shall see a part of the American munitions and aviation industry transferred across our
northern border into Canada, to the detriment of
American labor and to the impairment of an industry which is vitally important for our own
national defense. We must note, however regret-
fully, that war is the great laboratory in which in-
ventors and manufacturers obtain the experience
essential for perfecting their work.

Our people will willingly forego profits on arms
if that course would be for the general good. But a
program which may lead to a general increase in
armaments everywhere rather than a decrease,
which will automatically benefit strong nations and
make the weak weaker still, and which will handicap
to some extent at least our own national defense,
should certainly not commend itself to us unless the
off-setting reasons are compellingly strong.

There is a further consideration. If we propose
as part of our scheme of neutrality to maintain an

even-handed justice between the various belligerents, there is no reason why we should deprive the contestants who have control of the seas of the advantages which they may properly claim because of such control.

Let us face the issue frankly. The raising of the embargo on arms in the present European conflict would be of appreciable help to England and France and of no appreciable advantage to Germany, either in its present position or so long as Britain rules the seas. However, is it any of our business to deprive Britain of this advantage? Germany by creating superior land and air forces has been able to master Central Europe and take over the famous Skoda munition factories in Bohemia and the Polish industrial centers in Silesia. She has been able to secure these enormous benefits through the exercise of her military strength on land. Britain has chosen to develop another military weapon, her fleet. Subject only to the menace of the submarine, it gives her merchant marine access to the ports of the world and hence normally to the armament factories of the world, including those of the United States. There is a further element of Britain's power, and one which a neutral has no reason to try to diminish— namely, the financial resources which she has built up through her foreign trade. These, represented today by the foreign exchange assets of her nationals, would normally permit her to buy in the

world's markets. At the present time she controls
in this manner some two billion dollars' worth of
American securities alone, and through these she
should normally expect to be able to purchase from
neutrals the goods necessary for her to prosecute
a war.

We should be clear about this. To permit Britain
to use these elements of her strength is in no sense
unneutral. To deprive her of them is to hand her
antagonists a definite asset. Senator Borah says
that if we repealed the embargo we would "withhold"
arms from Germany; Senator Johnson says that repeal is undesirable because it would "favor" one side.
This is misleading. If by embargoing our foreign
trade and thus neutralizing the power attaching to
Britain's possession of a predominant fleet and a
strong financial position in foreign markets we feel
that we are advancing our national interests and
promoting our safety we are at liberty to take that
course. But if we do not feel that this would be
the result we are under no sort of compulsion so
to act in the name of anything remotely resembling
neutrality. Nothing whatsoever connected with any
conceivable duty as a neutral is involved. Nor
when partisans of the arms embargo extol its virtues
should we delude ourselves to the point of forgetting
that it applies to only one small segment of our
trade in war materials with belligerents. If the embargo is to insure the benefits which they suggest,

let them be consistent and extend it to cover cotton, copper, scrap iron and a multiplicity of other articles of export. The shock of that to our economy would be more than even the most isolationist Senator has so far wished to face frankly. Grass then would in truth grow in our streets, and social unrest would threaten all our institutions.

Nor should we forget that the 1937 Act is a statute of general application, hence that the arms embargo embodied in it does not apply solely to a European war. In Spain the arms embargo did not work as intended, and in the war in China the Administration did not apply it. What might be its effect in a war among South American countries? Most unfortunate, to put it mildly. It would seem extremely unwise for us to tie our hands in such a war, for by leaving European exporting countries to choose which of the Latin American belligerents to supply we might easily let them determine the result of the war. We have seen in Spain how the course of events can be altered by the abstention of certain countries from shipments of arms while other countries deliver their arms to one side only. We should hardly like to see the course of a war in this hemisphere determined by the governments which could control the activities of a Vickers-Armstrong, a Schneider-Creusot or a Krupp; and we ought not to tie ourselves to a course which makes that a possibility.   So long as the mandatory arms embargo remains in the 1937 Act we have done just that.

Just as she was invading hapless Poland, Soviet Russia defied the American idea of neutrality by formally notifying[2] both belligerents and neutrals, including the United States, that the Moscow Government "will pursue a policy of neutrality in relations between the U. S. S. R. and your country"— a strange communication indeed from one "neutral" to another! But unless the Administration decides that after all Soviet Russia is one of the belligerents, there is nothing in our law to prevent the Soviet Government from buying up airplanes originally ordered in this country by Britain and France, but which cannot be shipped to them because of the arms embargo, and using these planes to finish off anything that remains of Poland or perhaps extend the same form of "neutral" action into some other state. While under the specifications of the embargo the test of ultimate destination *should* prevent any planes sold to Soviet Russia, Italy or Japan from passing on to any of the belligerents, we may be pardoned a slight doubt that this rule could be enforced.   And even if it were enforced, the arrival of American planes evidently might at the least release Russian or Italian or Japanese planes for the use of some favored belligerent.   Powers are not particularly scrupulous when they go to war;

[2] *New York Times,* September 18, 1939.

and the Soviet Government would certainly chuckle if it could utilize our arms embargo to prolong the European chaos by acting as middleman for the distribution of our war material to the countries of its choice. How could we question the word of the "neutral" Soviet Government that it was purchasing solely for its own account?

The arms embargo should be eliminated from our neutrality legislation. This conclusion is reasonable apart from whatever views one may entertain about the merits of one cause or the other in the present European struggle. It will be urged, of course, that there may be difficulties and inconveniences in changing the law during the course of a conflict. Statements to this effect were made during the World War. But the embargo is not a part of international law; it is a self-denying ordinance which we adopt for our own convenience and can retract at our own pleasure. We should never hesitate, in time of war or in time of peace, to adopt the policy and pass the legislation which is best calculated to serve our national interests. To consider the Neutrality Law of 1937 as the last and final word on the subject of neutrality would be puerile. In the coming months or possibly years of conflict we may often find ourselves forced to change it. Let us demonstrate to the world now that we are not impotent or afraid to do so.

2. *Cash and Carry*

In discussing the arms embargo we pointed out that it applies only to so-called weapons of war, a limited part of the goods and commodities which belligerents want to buy from neutrals. Copper, cotton, oil, scrap iron and hundreds of other ingredients which go into the fabrication of arms and which are essential in modern war are not included. Proponents of the arms embargo who speak of it as a panacea to ward off all trouble mislead the public. They should not gloss over its very limited scope. If they were wholly frank they would have to admit that a sweeping cash and carry provision applicable to any and every kind of goods sold to belligerents—cotton and copper and oil as well as arms—would be more effective in eliminating incidents arising out of our trade relations with belligerents than an embargo solely on arms.

The reader will remember that the 1937 Neutrality Law originally contained both the arms embargo and the cash and carry provision, but that the latter expired on May 1, 1939. It can be restored only by new legislation. When Mr. Bernard M. Baruch brought forward the cash and carry idea in an article in *Today,* November 2, 1935, he said:

Under such policy all shipments of goods by Americans to belligerents would be embargoed, but we would be free to sell goods to any buyer who would send ships to our ports or charter our ships and take the goods away wholly at his own risk. We cannot become embroiled if we do that, in disputes of seizures and search, in rows over what is contraband and what is not. We cannot become indignant over losses because the losses are not ours.

Speaking before the Senate Foreign Relations Committee on April 6, 1939, Mr. Baruch described the plan in further detail:

It treats all nations alike. Each has an opportunity to get what it needs from us provided it takes title at the port of shipment, and provided, further, that the shipment is not made in American craft.

Of course, it is obvious that this will largely limit sales of supplies to those able to pay for them and able to move them, but, after all, the rule holds good in normal commerce. I do not see that we are required to adjust all inequalities of this sort. If that is our intention, we may as well face it and go to war. We discharge our obligations, including those to our long-term customers, by making available all of our products, just as we expect them to make available to us those supplies we need.[3]

Mr. Baruch does not itemize the "supplies we need" from, say, the British Empire. But it is suggestive to imagine what would be the surprised resentment among the American public if Britain said we could have our accustomed tin and rubber imports from British Malaya only in exchange for American airplanes.

Cash and carry has never yet been tried in time of war. We think it merits trial.

[3]*New York Times*, April 7, 1939.

3. *"Trade at Your Own Risk"*

When President Roosevelt on October 5, 1935, stated that American transactions of any character with either Italy or Ethiopia would be at the risk of the trader, he was breaking with the past. He was abandoning the policy of Jefferson and Wilson, and setting up a new relationship between the American trader and his government.

Admiral William S. Sims had already joined Mr. Charles Warren, Professor Philip C. Jessup and others in pointing the road along which the President now moved. Said Admiral Sims:

The point of the whole business is this: We cannot keep out of war and at the same time *enforce the freedom of the seas*—that is, the freedom to make profits out of countries in a death struggle. If a war arises, we must therefore choose between two courses: between great profits with grave risks of war on the one hand; or smaller profits and less risk on the other. . . .

And the time to decide is now, while we can think calmly and clearly, before war propaganda gets in its deadly work. . . .

Therefore, let every citizen who has the cause of honorable peace at heart take this stand: *Our trade as a neutral must be at the risk of the traders; our army and navy must not be used to protect this trade. It is a choice of profits or peace. Our country must remain at peace.*[4]

This policy of what might be called *caveat mercator*—let the trader beware—may help prevent

[4]Radio speech, May 8, 1935, reprinted in pamphlet form by World Peace Foundation.

incidents likely to engage our national interests. And it would have the advantage of not establishing irrevocable precedents, as happens when hard-and-fast rules are given legislative enactment. Of course it would not eliminate the difficulty of determining the line between legitimate trade with other neutrals and trade ultimately destined for a belligerent. That difficulty is inherent in any attempt to regulate trade in time of war.

No legislation by Congress is required to adopt the "trade at your own risk" policy. The Executive, which is authorized to conduct American foreign relations, can put it into effect at any time. Had we adopted it in 1914, the ensuing years might have told a different story. Most of our initial troubles with Britain would have been avoided. Germany could not have complained that we had bowed to the British blockade and forced her to abandon her own. On the other hand, the sinking of American vessels and the loss of American lives would have occurred despite the Executive warning, and these would have tended in any event to arouse American opinion. And what if Germany had sent her submarines across the Atlantic and sunk our ships at our very doors? That might happen today. It is useless to speculate whether the "trade at your own risk" policy would have kept us out of the last war. All that can be said is that it merits a thorough trial in the present crisis, unless Congress meanwhile enacts cash and carry legislation.

Obviously we must protect ourselves against the possibility that this policy might be seized on by our commercial rivals to sweep our trade from the seas and substitute their own. During the World War it was sometimes suggested by our harassed traders that the British blockade was used in that way. The Executive therefore must be left in a position to see to it that no improper advantage is taken of our traders because of the belief that they are not to have the Government's support in case they get into trouble. The policy must mean that interference with American traders may be tolerated only if it is incident to the actual conduct of hostilities. We cannot allow it to be interpreted as meaning that we would remain quiescent in other circumstances, or that we would be precluded from presenting a bill for damages after the war—if a solvent belligerent could then be found.

4. *Moral Suasion*

In their efforts to keep the United States out of foreign entanglements, President Roosevelt and Secretary Hull have on occasion combined the "trade at your own risk" policy with attempts to influence American traders to refrain voluntarily from trade with belligerents. Their action along the latter line, usually referred to as "moral suasion," has already been described in our accounts of the Ethiopian war, the war in Spain and the Japanese war in China.

During the Ethiopian war, on November 15, 1935—about a month after the President said that transactions with either Italy or Ethiopia would be at the risk of the trader—Secretary Hull made the following statement:

The American people are entitled to know that there are certain commodities such as oil, copper, trucks, tractors, scrap iron, and scrap steel which are essential war materials, although not actually "arms, ammunition, or implements of war," and that according to recent government trade reports a considerably increased amount of these is being exported for war purposes. This class of trade is directly contrary to the policy of this Government as announced in official statements of the President and Secretary of State, as it is also contrary to the general spirit of the recent neutrality act.

Secretary Hull adopted this monitory attitude in order—partly at any rate—to forestall any clash between the United States and the members of the League, then engaged in elaborating a system of sanctions for use against Italy.

If our trade is to be restricted, we think it should be by law, or under a "trade at your own risk" policy, and not by moral pressure, which may influence the honest and high-minded trader and throw whatever business he renounces into the hands of less scrupulous competitors. Further, we can imagine cases in which moral arguments would not be effective. For example, they would have no influence whatever upon the agents of belligerents, who either directly or through corporations organized for the purpose might continue to export articles, while American citizens, bowing to the Executive's wishes, refrained.

In certain limited spheres of activity the Government, through the control which it exercises over government-subsidized agencies, particularly shipping, might be able to influence trade with belligerents without further legislation. We have discussed this already in the section on the war in China. There might be further instances—for example, in the oil industry—where the Government could bring about a voluntary agreement in harmony with its wishes. Control of most of the available tankers lies in a rather small number of hands; the oil companies might be induced to agree that none of their tankers should be used in a particular trade which the Government felt was contrary to its policy and likely to jeopardize the national safety and welfare. In the field of financing, the Government in the early days of 1914 and at other times has effectively intervened to prevent or control the making of loans to foreign governments, even though no legislative prohibitions existed.

The President at all times has the right to determine the usefulness and necessity of extending protection to our citizens, or of withholding it; and he can warn them in advance that in certain situations he would withhold it. But to restrict American foreign trade by moral pressure seems, generally speaking, to attempt to graft a new idea onto our domestic law, and to stop American citizens from carrying on, even inside the United States, activities which are legally open to them. The necessity or wisdom of this is not clear.

5. Quotas

In view of the obvious impossibility of putting a total embargo on all materials useful in war, a suggestion has been put forward that we limit our exports to belligerents to the average peacetime trade. In other words, we might try to distinguish between the normal trade and the abnormal "war profiteering" trade.

This sounds excellent in theory; but in practice it would be almost impossible of application. To be effective, a quota system would require a strict regimentation and rationing of our exports between clamoring groups of exporters. Our authorities not only would have to fix quotas for belligerents, but also for all countries in the general war area and for all countries that might serve as transshipment centers. For example, in case we tried to ration shipments to Great Britain, we should probably find other countries—Canada and Mexico, for example—increasing their purchases and sending the goods on to Great Britain, with no result except to increase the cost to the purchaser and to hand over the carrying trade to the vessels of other nations. It is true that during the World War we rationed our shipments to Germany's neutral neighbors; we also rationed all our most important exports to *all* countries and restricted imports from nearly all countries. But to accomplish our aim we had at our disposal a most elaborate wartime machinery, in a time when the United States and the Allies were in complete control of the seas, and when if the neutrals had evidenced a lack of coöperation we should merely have starved them back to a reasonable frame of mind. It would be a highly difficult and complicated undertaking to apply a quota system unless the United States was itself at war and willing to submit to a painful degree of regimentation—and then only in coöperation with other great maritime Powers.

6. *Loans and Credits*

The so-called Johnson Act, passed April 13, 1934,[5] bans the flotation of further loans in this country (except refunding loans and possibly the borrowing involved in ordinary banking and commercial transactions) by governments or govern-

[5]Text in Appendix 3.

ment agencies which are not paying interest on their debts to the Government of the United States. This eliminates the major European Powers as potential borrowers. Japan was not among the nations thus excluded from the American financial market; nor did the Act cut off private industrial companies or munition factories in the countries which are excluded.

When the Neutrality Act of 1935 was amended early in 1936 it included for the first time a provision banning public loans to any belligerent state or to any of its political subdivisions or to any individual or institution acting on its behalf, effective whenever the President issues a proclamation under the Act. The President was given the authority to except "ordinary commercial credits and short-time obligations in aid of legal transactions and of a character customarily used in normal peacetime commercial transactions." Further, the prohibition was not to apply to a "renewal or adjustment of such indebtedness as may exist on the date of the President's proclamation." The Neutrality Act of 1937 contains similar provisions, and these were brought into effect by the President's proclamation on September 6, 1939.[6]

Ray Stannard Baker's biography of Wilson reminds us what perplexities were caused during the

[6]For text see Appendix 13.

World War by this problem of loans and credits.[7]
At the outset Secretary Bryan opposed loans
to the belligerents, holding that money was
"the worst of all contrabands because it com-
mands everything else." He felt that the powerful
financial interests which would be connected with
loans would use their influence through the press
and otherwise to support the governments whose
loans they had floated. Mr. Lansing, then Coun-
sellor of the State Department, supported Secretary
Bryan's view that it was wise to discourage "the
money of this country from taking part in a foreign
war." Consequently, on August 15, 1914, Messrs.
J. P. Morgan & Co. were advised that in the judgment of the Government "loans by American bankers to any foreign nation which is at war are inconsistent with the true spirit of neutrality." There
was, of course, no legal ban on loans; but the mere
statement of government policy was sufficient to
prevent their flotation at that time.

Not much more than a year was needed to bring
about an entire change in this policy. Principles
and theories, very likely correct in the abstract, gave
way to the hard reality that American trade with
the Allies was increasing and that to hold that trade
we had to finance it from the moment the credit balance of the Allies on this side of the Atlantic was
exhausted. The first breach in the policy related to

[7]"Life and Letters of Woodrow Wilson," v. 5, p. 175 *et seq.*

commercial credits as distinct from what were then called "general loans," that is, loans floated for sale to the general public. Before the end of 1914, inquiring bankers were advised that the warning against loans did not apply to ordinary credit facilities for the shipments of goods to belligerents. A banking credit of $10,000,000 was arranged by France, followed in March of 1915 by a publicly offered one-year French "note issue." At the same time (March 31, 1915) the change in policy was elaborated in an announcement by the State Department.

In his letter to Senator Stone, dated January 20, 1915, Secretary Bryan, with the approval of President Wilson, had already defended the differentiation between public and private loans on the ground that private commercial transactions did not arouse any "general spirit of partisanship."[8] Public loans were still discouraged on the ground that they "would be taken up chiefly by those who are in sympathy with the belligerent seeking the loan," and that "the people would be divided into groups of partisans, which would result in intense bitterness and might cause an undesirable, if not a serious, situation."

A chart of American industrial activity in the period since 1854, prepared by Colonel Leonard

[8]"Foreign Relations of the United States," 1914, Supplement, p. xii.

Ayres, shows that there was a severe depression in the United States from the outbreak of the World War until about halfway through 1915. But by August 1915 the flood of Allied buying orders in the United States had reached a point where the rising trend had carried business from below "normal" up into the "prosperity" zone. Private banking credits were no longer adequate; and it became a question either of cutting down on the orders, and facing the economic difficulties which would result, or lifting the ban on loans. The ban was lifted. In September 1915 the first great long-term Anglo-French loan was publicly offered in the United States.[9]

The story of the lifting of the ban has now been made public and is of sufficient significance to be repeated here. In writing to President Wilson on August 25, 1915, the Secretary of State pointed out that conditions had materially changed since the autumn of 1914 when the flotation of any general loan by a belligerent had been discouraged.[10] He

[9]The story of how the Allies (Great Britain, France, Russia and Italy) paid for the goods which they imported from the United States from the outbreak of the World War up to the time of our entry in April 1917 was told in a memorandum submitted by J. P. Morgan and Co. to the Senate Munitions Committee inquiry (Nye Committee) in January 1936 (see *New York Times,* January 7, 1936). The value of these imports (which of course included all goods and not solely war materials) was about $7,000,000,000. This sum was balanced as follows: paid for by exports to America and normal invisible items, about $1,600,000,000; paid for by gold, $1,100,000,000; paid for by liquidation of short-term American debts abroad, estimated by U. S. Treasury as exceeding $500,000,000; paid for by sale of securities and other assets, $1,400,000,000; paid for by pledge of securities (collateral loans), $1,400,000,000; paid for by unsecured loans, not to exceed $1,000,000,000; total $7,000,000,000.

[10]*New York Times,* January 10, 1936.

noted that the question of exchange and the large debts resulting from purchases by belligerents required some method of funding these debts in this country. President Wilson's reply the next day favored a government stand which "would take no action either for or against such a transaction." His letter was somewhat vague and apparently the Secretary of State felt that it was important to go into the matter more fully. On September 6, 1915, Mr. Lansing sent the President a detailed written description of the financial situation of the country, in which he gave the opinion that a change in policy on loans to the belligerents was desirable. He showed that for the year 1915 the excess of our exports over imports was approximately two and one-half billion dollars, that the sums of gold available for use by the foreign purchasers (without disastrously affecting their credit), plus their foreign securities and other assets, were not sufficient to meet their unfavorable trade balance; and that unless financial means were found a great shrinkage of our export trade would occur. The result, he said, would be "industrial depression, idle capital, idle labor, numerous failures, financial demoralization, general unrest and suffering among the labor classes." He put this concluding question to the President: "Can we afford to let a declaration as to our conception of 'the true spirit of neutrality' made in the first days of the war stand in the way of our national interests, which seem to be seriously threatened?" The final decision was in the negative.

We have here an illuminating example of what would be the likely trend of events in any great foreign war. It is easy to state the theory that we should separate ourselves entirely from the rest of the world when the world goes to war. But as the economic results of such a policy become apparent the pressure to reverse it becomes very strong. To say this is not to imply that there was or would be any deep-dyed plot by American bankers. What happened in 1915 was an ordinary case of the working of economic law once an abnormal wartime trade had been allowed to develop.

Any system of protective neutrality can properly attempt to head off this trend. To buy the bonds of a belligerent is to gamble on his success; the psychological results may be bad; and the effect on the financial condition of the country after the war is over may be unfortunate through stimulating mushroom wartime industries.

The American public, as a recent Gallup poll showed, likes the ban on public financing by belligerents which is contained in the present Neutrality Act. There certainly is no reason why any change should be made now in these provisions of the Act, unless to stop up loopholes. The law as presently drafted does not make clear whether public loans to a private industrial company—Vickers-Armstrong, for example—are barred. While such a loan could hardly be floated except with some kind of a government guarantee, or what amounted to a government guarantee, it is clear that if we prevent a belligerent government from borrowing we should likewise prevent any corporation or citizen of a belligerent country from doing the same thing.

The exception which is permitted in the case of commercial credits or short-term obligations in aid of normal commercial transactions is probably necessary and desirable as long as commercial relations are carried on with belligerents; and certainly we are not advocating here any attempt to revert to the ill-fated Jeffersonian program of a complete trade embargo. Any undue extension of banking credit to cover trade with belligerents would probably be controlled to a considerable extent by the Federal Reserve Board. In addition, the amount to which such credits would be extended is further limited by the marketable collateral or other security which belligerents might be able to furnish to the banks making the loans.

But legislation of this character creates many problems. For example, our northern neighbor Canada, its provinces and its municipalities have normally done a considerable amount of their financing in the American market. Quite apart from any need for wartime loans, they would in any case look to the United States as a natural and important source of new capital for the development of their resources and to refund maturing loans contracted here and in England. Possibly the exemption noted in the law for renewals or adjustments of existing indebtedness would cover a new loan the proceeds of which were exclusively devoted to refunding a maturing loan. It is to be hoped that any regulations or interpretations of this section of the Act will take this problem into account.

7. Collections of Funds and Activities of Foreign Agents

In its anxiety to thwart every possible activity that might arouse popular feeling in this country over the actions of a belligerent, and hence perhaps become what is now called propaganda (meaning something evil), Congress decided to bar the solicitation or receipt of funds for belligerent governments. A provision to this effect was made a part of section 3 of the Neutrality Act of 1937. Exception was made, however, for the collection by non-governmental agencies of funds for medical aid or for food and clothing to relieve human suffering. Such permissible collections, however, are subject to the approval of the President and to the rules and regulations prescribed by him.[11]

[11]For the text of the regulations governing the collection of such funds in the present European war see Appendix 12.

In June 1938 Congress took another and probably more effective step toward restricting foreign propaganda by requiring the registration of persons employed by foreign governments for propaganda purposes in the United States.[12] Although this Act does not expressly refer to war or neutrality, it may be of some significance in controlling belligerent propaganda. Under its provisions, those acting here as public-relations counsel or agents for a foreign principal are required to register and to file certain information with the Secretary of State. Exception is made, of course, for foreign diplomatic and consular officers, and likewise for persons, other than public-relations counsel or publicity agents, "performing only private, non-political, financial, mercantile, or other activities in furtherance of the bona fide trade or commerce of such foreign principal." In other words, the Act is intended to disclose the activities of political and publicity agents and not to interfere with normal commercial or cultural activities. But in practice the line is sometimes hard to draw.

8. *Travel on Belligerent Vessels and Travel in War Zones*

One feature of all the neutrality legislation introduced since 1935 has been a restriction on American

[12]Pub. No. 583, 75th Cong., June 8, 1938. See also Department of State Press Releases, September 10, 1938, for the regulations under the Act.

travel on belligerent vessels. We had our experience of the risks of this travel in the World War, and have wanted to prevent our neutrality from being unnecessarily jeopardized again by the loss of American lives at the hands of belligerents, particularly through submarine activities.

The 1935 Neutrality Act, as amended in 1936, stipulated that American citizens thenceforth traveled on belligerent vessels at their own risk. In 1937 the provision was changed. Such travel was made definitely "unlawful," and (as in other sections of the Act) violators were made liable to a fine of $10,000, or to imprisonment for not more than five years, or both. The travel prohibition was not to come into effect for citizens returning to the United States until ninety days after the date of the President's proclamation of neutrality and was subject to Executive regulations.

The wisdom of making it a crime to travel on the ships of nations at war rather than to be content with a warning and a disavowal of responsibility is open to question. Would judges and juries impose fines or jail sentences for offenses of this sort, however the law is worded? Shades of the prohibition law, and of other laws that seem to go beyond what the public conscience approves, rise up with a warning. In a great emergency there may well be cases when conscientious American citizens will feel themselves forced to act in a manner contrary to this provision of the law. They will be willing to assume the risk involved and will ask no one to take any responsibility for their act. It seems unnecessary to place them in the dilemma of failing to carry out what may seem to them a larger duty than any involved in refraining from travel on the vessel of a belligerent, and thereby becoming a criminal.

In any case, if the provision about travel on ships of belligerents is to stand, the experience of the past few weeks suggests that it ought to come into effect more promptly. The very fact that the statute left ninety days in which American citizens might avail themselves of non-neutral ships to return home shows its unrealistic nature. Under conditions of modern warfare the first ninety days are fully as likely to produce unfortunate incidents as any other period.

The sinking of the *Athenia* is a case in point. The comparative calm with which news of this tragedy was received in the United States merely indicates the change in public opinion about incidents of this character since the days of the *Lusitania*. American hostility towards Germany is certainly much greater today than it was on May 7, 1915. The *Athenia* was homeward bound and could not have been carrying munitions or other contraband. Germany had given no warning against the use of the vessel. Are we to conclude that isolated instances of savagery which do not necessarily indicate the settled governmental policy of a belligerent will to-day leave American sentiment relatively unaffected? Possibly American public opinion is shell shocked by all that it has read about events in Europe and the Far East during the past few years; perhaps its capacity for horror, pity and resentment is exhausted. Obviously, however, an isolated case like the *Athenia* has much less effect than a second outrage would have. Public anger would rise in arithmetical progression. But it probably would be aroused in some degree whenever submarines attack passenger vessels without warning and without making any attempt to see that the lives of passengers are saved, even if those passengers are not American but are English or Dutch or French or Scandinavian.

Americans should not travel on the ships of belligerents except at their own personal risk. But to try to keep them off by threats of fines and jail is not likely to be effective, and it is not likely to make American opinion indifferent to the continued ruthless destruction of human lives on passenger vessels of any nationality.

The prompt arming and convoying of the passenger vessels of belligerents used by Americans during the ninety-day period of grace apparently created a worrisome problem for our officials. The distraught Americans who had already actually embarked on the *Aquitania* at Southampton on September 8, 1939, for the voyage to America were required to listen to a last-minute lecture on international law from the local American Consul, acting upon instructions from Ambassador Kennedy. The Ambassador told puzzled passengers that "it is his duty to warn American citizens taking passage on vessels of belligerent nations, that when such vessels are being convoyed the opposing belligerent may claim the right to sink them without warning." The Ambassador's statement was made "to acquaint Americans with a contingency which might conceivably arise." It was not a comforting send-off. The Ambassador did not enter into the even more complex question of the status of "armed merchantmen." But the *Aquitania* arrived in New York with two businesslike 12-pound guns mounted on her stern, and international lawyers took down their dusty tomes to re-read the endless debates on this subject from the days of our neutrality in the last World War.

9. *Areas of Combat Operations*

Another plan was broached in the discussion of how to protect American shipping from the depredations of states at war. Before Congress ad-

journed in August 1939 the suggestion was made
that the President be given authority to define areas
of combat operations into which neither American
vessels nor American citizens would be allowed to
enter. The plan died, along with other proposed
amendments to the 1937 Act, when the Senate refused to give them consideration and Congress adjourned. In the House of Representatives the idea
of a "proscribed area" had encountered serious
opposition on the ground that it gave the President
too great discretion. There was an obvious fear
that the Executive might permit American trade
with one belligerent and deny it to another by the
manner in which he laid out the limits of the danger
zone.

10. *Executive Discretion*

The reluctance of Congress to grant the President authority to define danger zones was typical of
a feeling which is broad and deep. Congress had
first refused to permit the Executive to apply the
arms embargo unilaterally to one belligerent—
rightly, we believe. But having won this battle, and
tasted Roosevelt blood, Congress then proceeded (as
we have already seen) to narrow discretionary authority in fields where some should properly be
given.

Congress hoped to avoid letting the President decide when legislation to restrict our trade should go into effect; but here it was only partially successful, since the President was left with the power to proclaim the existence of a state of war. There is no legal means to force him to make such a proclamation. The only remedy is impeachment.

Under the cash and carry provisions as they appeared in the 1937 Act, the President had authority to determine whether American safety and interests required that they be invoked and also to determine what articles were to be on a cash basis. But the cash and carry provisions did not remain long in effect. The President also was given some authority to determine what form of commercial credits could be granted to belligerents. So much for the discretion allowed him. It certainly amounts to very little.

If Congress is ready to take the responsibility of legislating *ad hoc* to meet each and every particular situation as it arises, and is prepared to remain continuously in session for that purpose, and thinks this is an effective way of conducting foreign policy, then it can reduce the degree of discretion left the Executive to a minimum. If Congress today desires to legislate specifically to meet the problems of the present European war, facing the risks that drastic and unpredictable changes will occur in it as it proceeds, Executive discretion can be almost eliminated. For example, Congress could now legislate a cash and carry program and enumerate each and every article to be covered.

But the difficulties and risks of that course must be evident to anyone who thinks twice. And when Congress proposes to legislate in general for all wars, present and future, it should pause to study the experience of the past. Then it will realize that in this field the legislation of today is the headache of tomorrow. It would be far better to repeal the entire 1937 Act, with the exception of the Munitions Control Board and certain purely technical features, and revert to our old position, than to have on our statute books a law which leaves the Executive no discretion whatsoever.

On the whole, we are willing to accept at the outset the premise that the Executive must be allowed liberty of action, within certain limits, to conduct the foreign relations of the United States in periods when other nations are at war just as he is accorded that liberty when the world is at peace. There is no alternative to giving him this discretion if we are to have a sensible and constructive foreign policy under either condition. As between the risk that the Executive may possibly abuse this discretion and the risk inherent in a policy which ties the Executive with legislative restrictions in the conduct of foreign policy, the former alternative seems to us preferable. The Constitutional safeguards which already limit Executive action will remain. When we go beyond these, and try to legislate in advance on details of foreign policy, we run the risk of forcing the Administration to embark on a course which, in unforeseen and absolutely unforeseeable situations, may lead toward war rather than peace, and handicap rather than help those who are trying to protect our real national interests.

There has been much talk about the patriotic duty to forget partisan politics in this time of crisis and danger. We cannot help feeling that if this were in fact done, some of the imagined obstacles to allowing the Executive to fulfill its natural and proper function in the day-by-day conduct of foreign policy would disappear.

11. *Referendum on War*

Not unconnected with the efforts to "legislate peace" have been various attempts to amend the Constitution by inserting a provision requiring a popular referendum before Congress could declare war (except in cases of actual invasion). The theory is that this kind of constitutional requirement would prevent the Government from involving the country in foreign wars against the will of the people. It betrays a lack of confidence in the honesty or good judgment of the representatives whom the people elect, and a vast confidence that popular psychology is always calm and public action always deliberate.

The best-known attempt of this sort was the resolution introduced by Representative Ludlow of Indiana on February 5, 1937. The Administration opposed it, and on January 10, 1938, the House, by a vote of 209 to 188, refused to take it out of committee for consideration on the floor. The opponents of the resolution have pointed out that, far from achieving its avowed purpose, a constitutional amendment requiring a referendum in a moment of great international crisis would endanger the security of the United States by crippling the conduct of its foreign relations and by emphasizing internal differences. Attempts to conduct the foreign relations of a great nation like the United States by popular referenda would not be feasible even in an era of international good will. The idea seems almost childishly naïve today, when several of the Great Powers are governed by régimes which conduct their foreign policies by strokes of lightning.

Aside from the fact that the project repudiates our system of democratic representative government, it fails even as a peace plan. The Ludlow resolution would permit war by a simple plurality. But Congress would never vote a war resolution if it thought that a mere 51 percent of the people were favorable; it would act only if absolutely convinced of the support of the overwhelming majority of the people. Let us trust the sobriety, good judgment and responsiveness to public will of our elected representatives to keep us at peace so long as our national interests permit.

12. *Hemisphere Solidarity*

It has been the policy of the Roosevelt Administration to emphasize the concern of the United States with the peace and security of all the countries of this hemisphere. In a sense this policy is nothing but a reaffirmation of the principles of the Monroe Doctrine—but a Doctrine restated expressly to cover Canada. In his address at Kingston, Ontario, on August 18, 1938, President Roosevelt declared that "the people of the United States will not stand idly by if domination of Canadian soil is threatened by any other empire." He dramatically reaffirmed the assurance on September 12, 1939, after Canada had gone to war against Germany, thus in effect making the United States a guarantor of one of the belligerents.

Yet the efforts of the United States have not been confined to a reaffirmation of the unilateral policy given expression in the Monroe Doctrine. At the Inter-American Conference for the Maintenance of Peace at Buenos Aires in December 1936 the delegation of the United States urged the adoption of a convention[13] which would have set up a Permanent Inter-American Consultative Committee to watch over the carrying out of Inter-American engagements for the peaceful settlement of international disputes and likewise of the scheme set forth in the proposed convention for a "common and solidary attitude" in case of war between American republics. There was to be a mandatory and impartial embargo on arms shipments to the belligerents, and the floating of loans by the belligerents in the neutral republics was to be prohibited. The scheme obviously reflected the provisions of the Neutrality Act as it then stood on the statute books of the United States. But why did the Administration, which never was enthusiastic about the arms embargo, try to export it to Latin America, even though it was not to apply to non-American wars? In the end, the scheme failed of adoption, and so did the proposal for a permanent consultative body. But another draft convention proposed by the United States delegation was adopted, with only a few changes, as the Convention for the Maintenance, Preservation and Reëstablishment of Peace (December 23, 1936). It provides for mutual consultations between the American Republics in case of war or threat of war in America, while

in the event of an international war outside America which might menace the peace of the American Republics, such con-

[13]Department of Sate Press Releases, December 12, 1936.

sultation shall also take place to determine the proper time and manner in which the signatory states, if they so desire, may eventually coöperate in some action tending to preserve the peace of the American Continent.

At Lima, in December 1938, the Eighth International Conference of American States reaffirmed the "continental solidarity" of the American States and provided for consultation in case of threats to the peace, security or territorial integrity of any American Republic. This declaration, known as the "Declaration of Lima," marked a definite step toward converting the Monroe Doctrine into a common policy of all the American nations.

It was in accord with these 1936 and 1938 provisions for consultation that a call was issued early in September 1939 for a conference of the American States to meet at Panama on September 21 for the purpose of discussing the possible effects of the European war on the position of the American nations. The invitation was issued jointly by eight of the nations, including the United States.

We need hardly point out that the course pursued by the United States in regard to "hemisphere solidarity," while undoubtedly designed to foster the security and vital national interest of this country, does not mean the avoidance of involvement, at any price, in the conflicts of foreign nations. As a matter of fact, the chances of such involvement are increased by the self-imposed burden of protecting other American countries. The policy of "hemisphere solidarity," based primarily on considerations of our own interests, is opposed to the doctrine of isolation and neutrality at any price.

The policy, especially in its application to Canada, meets a serious obstacle in our neutrality legislation. How can our professed concern with the security of Canada be reconciled with the imposition of an arms embargo against that country when —as at present—it is involved in war? Already Canadian newspapers have been asking, some reproachfully, some indignantly, what the "good neighbor" policy means when limited by a neutrality act which prevents Canadians from buying needed airplanes in the United States while American exporters technically remain free to sell them to Soviet Russia or Japan or Italy.

It has already been pointed out how the application of the arms embargo in cases of war between American republics might facilitate the growth of European political influences in those republics through the supplying of arms by European states. We may add that rigid statutory restrictions on trade with belligerents might conceivably lead to the undermining of the economic position of the United States in the Western Hemisphere and set at nought all our recent efforts to promote trade with our neighbors, including, of course, Canada—next to Britain herself our best customer.

13. *Traditional Neutrality*

In view of the difficulties and risks of hard-and-fast neutrality legislation, the suggestion is sometimes made that it all should be swept away and that we should return to the "old" neutrality and to "international law." Talk of this was revived when the President issued two proclamations on the outbreak of the present war in Europe, one under the old neutrality statute, built up from the days of Washington and revised in 1917, and the other under the neutrality legislation which we have been discussing in these pages, namely, the arms and loan embargoes and the restrictions on shipping and travel. As between rigid prohibitions such as the arms embargo and a return to the "old" neutrality, certainly the latter is preferable. But if by returning to the old neutrality we mean that we should again attempt to assert rights of trade and travel under some theory that such rights exist in international law, and if we think that therefore we shall automatically see those rights respected by other Powers, then we deceive ourselves. If we wish to enforce those rights we must use our Army and Navy.

CHAPTER VIII

AMERICA CANNOT LEGISLATE PEACE

WE HAVE reached the end of our brief appraisal of the various legislative methods adopted or suggested for helping keep the United States out of war. We have argued them, pro and con, in the light of past experience. If that experience proves anything, it is that the only way for us to be absolutely sure of escaping entanglement in foreign wars is for there to be no wars. There is no difficulty in keeping clear of wars between minor states; but even minor wars easily become major wars. Today each one of us must be aware of the difficulties—hardships perhaps—involved in staying out of a war in which, in one form or another, practically every other Great Power is engaged. Even those who count most heavily on neutrality legislation to keep the United States at peace must realize that perhaps they are mistaken, that there is at least a chance that their magic formulæ will not work. If this is true, then the elaboration of a complicated system of safeguards to protect American neutrality cannot be the sole aim of American policy.

The Government, both in its executive and legislative branches, has a continuing responsibility which is broader than the determination to escape from some particular difficulty or danger. There is a direct national interest that hostilities should not occur anywhere and that when they do occur they be brought to the earliest end possible. And there is also a direct national interest that out of such widespread turmoil as now prevails, with such a universal dislocation of political, commercial, financial and cultural relations, men should find some better way than war to settle their national disputes.

We speak of American responsibility with diffidence. The word has been overworked and is unpopular. But the responsibility is there, because we are a great nation, magnificently endowed with natural resources, almost a continent in ourselves, fortunately situated between two oceans. In conformity with the civilized principle that power confers responsibility, it has been our duty to support any reasonable move to organize the world more effectively for peace. Some would argue that we have adequately fulfilled that duty from 1918 until today; others that in some particulars we have been remiss; others that it would have been of no avail even if we had done more. However this may be, we still have a duty to help limit the scope and duration of the present conflict. This is not a duty owing from the United States to other nations; it is a duty which our Government owes to its people and which we owe to ourselves. That during the past twenty years we should have reserved independence of judgment and refused to accept international commitments regarding our political course of action in unforeseen future situations was prudent and in conformity with our traditions. By analogy, we feel it was not prudent for Congress to put the strait-jacket of mandatory neutrality legislation on our course of action in unforeseen situations. Isolation is not a lasting and sufficient shield for American interests. And it was reckless to think that it could be made so by legislation.

Americans do not seem to us to be in a moral position to blame the present chaos in the world on everybody but themselves. Those who fought every specific course of action which aimed to establish a new world order, arguing that the United States should play no part, carry their share of the blame. Overlooking our country's influence and power, they were unwilling to take the slightest risks for peace. Today the greater part of the world is at war again, and it would be a brave man who said we were not more entangled than ever.

As previous chapters have attempted to show, there are certain specific ways in which our legislators can restrict the actions of our citizens in time of war so that they do not unnecessarily engage the honor, prestige or interests of the nation as a whole. But no neutrality legislation can give us the advantages of an isolation which does not in fact exist, and those who preach the contrary are not, we believe, the realists they call themselves.

Since the beginning of the present European conflict the American public have been advised to keep their emotions under control. Their restraint so far has been admirable. But to recommend coolness is not to recommend indifference. The most weighty judgment is deliberate. A cause to which we incline emotionally is not for that reason wrong any more than it is for that reason right. We have said that the country should be slow to anger and should judge the acts of foreign governments in the light of our own national interests. This does not mean that Americans count the preservation of liberty here and the survival of human liberties in other countries as of only trifling importance in a world largely given over to *Machtpolitik*. It would be a stupid foreign ruler indeed who thought so.

APPENDICES

APPENDIX 1

PRESIDENT WILSON'S PROCLAMATION OF NEUTRALITY, AUGUST 4, 1914[1]

Whereas, a state of war unhappily exists between Austria-Hungary and Servia and between Germany and Russia and between Germany and France;[2] And Whereas the United States is on terms of friendship and amity with the contending powers, and with the persons inhabiting their several dominions;

And Whereas there are citizens of the United States residing within the territories or dominions of each of the said belligerents and carrying on commerce, trade, or other business or pursuits therein;

And Whereas there are subjects of each of the said belligerents residing within the territory or jurisdiction of the United States, and carrying on commerce, trade, or other business or pursuits therein;

And Whereas the laws and treaties of the United States, without interfering with the free expression of opinion and sympathy, or with the commercial manufacture or sale of arms or munitions of war, nevertheless impose upon all persons who may be within their territory and jurisdiction the duty of an impartial neutrality during the existence of the contest;

And Whereas it is the duty of a neutral government not to permit or suffer the making of its waters subservient to the purposes of war;

Now, Therefore, I, Woodrow Wilson, President of the United States of America, in order to preserve the neutrality

[1]"Papers Relating to the Foreign Relations of the United States," 1914, Supplement, The World War, p. 547-51.

[2]Additional proclamations identical in character were subsequently issued for the war between Germany and Great Britain, Austria-Hungary and Russia, etc., etc.

of the United States and of its citizens and of persons within its territory and jurisdiction, and to enforce its laws and treaties, and in order that all persons, being warned of the general tenor of the laws and treaties of the United States in this behalf, and of the law of nations, may thus be prevented from any violation of the same, do hereby declare and proclaim that by certain provisions of the act approved on the 4th day of March, A. D. 1909, commonly known as the "Penal Code of the United States" the following acts are forbidden to be done, under severe penalties, within the territory and jurisdiction of the United States, to-wit:—

1. Accepting and exercising a commission to serve either of the said belligerents by land or by sea against the other belligerent.

2. Enlisting or entering into the service of either of the said belligerents as a soldier, or as a marine, or seaman on board of any vessel of war, letter of marque, or privateer.

3. Hiring or retaining another person to enlist or enter himself in the service of either of the said belligerents as a soldier, or as a marine, or seaman on board of any vessel of war, letter of marque, or privateer.

4. Hiring another person to go beyond the limits or jurisdiction of the United States with intent to be enlisted as aforesaid.

5. Hiring another person to go beyond the limits of the United States with intent to be entered into service as aforesaid.

6. Retaining another person to go beyond the limits of the United States with intent to be enlisted as aforesaid.

7. Retaining another person to go beyond the limits of the United States with intent to be entered into service as aforesaid. (But the said act is not to be construed to extend to a citizen or subject of either belligerent who, being tran-

siently within the United States, shall, on board of any vessel of war, which, at the time of its arrival within the United States, was fitted and equipped as such vessel of war, enlist or enter himself or hire or retain another subject or citizen of the same belligerent, who is transiently within the United States, to enlist or enter himself to serve such belligerent on board such vessel of war, if the United States shall then be at peace with such belligerent.)

8. Fitting out and arming, or attempting to fit out and arm, or procuring to be fitted out and armed, or knowingly being concerned in the furnishing, fitting out, or arming of any ship or vessel with intent that such ship or vessel shall be employed in the service of either of the said belligerents.

9. Issuing or delivering a commission within the territory or jurisdiction of the United States for any ship or vessel to the intent that she may be employed as aforesaid.

10. Increasing or augmenting, or procuring to be increased or augmented, or knowingly being concerned in increasing or augmenting, the force of any ship of war, cruiser, or other armed vessel, which at the time of her arrival within the United States was a ship of war, cruiser, or armed vessel in the service of either of the said belligerents, or belonging to the subjects of either, by adding to the number of guns of such vessels, or by changing those on board of her for guns of a larger calibre, or by the addition thereto of any equipment solely applicable to war.

11. Beginning or setting on foot or providing or preparing the means for any military expedition or enterprise to be carried on from the territory or jurisdiction of the United States against the territories or dominions of either of the said belligerents.

And I do hereby further declare and proclaim that any frequenting and use of the waters within the territorial jurisdiction of the United States by the armed vessels of a belligerent, whether public ships or privateers, for the purpose of preparing for hostile operations, or as posts of observation upon the ships of war or privateers or merchant vessels of a belligerent lying within or being about to enter the juris-diction of the United States, must be regarded as unfriendly and offensive, and in violation of that neutrality which it is the determination of this government to observe; and to the end that the hazard and inconvenience of such apprehended practices may be avoided, I further proclaim and declare that from and after the fifth day of August instant, and during the continuance of the present hostilities between Austria-Hungary and Servia, and Germany and Russia, and Germany and France, no ship of war or privateer of any belligerent shall be permitted to make use of any port, harbor, roadstead, or water subject to the jursdiction of the United States from which a vessel of an opposing belligerent (whether the same shall be a ship of war, a privateer, or a merchant ship) shall have previously departed, until after the expiration of at least twenty-four hours from the departure of such last-mentioned vessel beyond the jurisdiction of the United States.

If any ship of war or privateer of a belligerent shall, after the time this notification takes effect, enter any port, harbor, roadstead, or waters of the United States, such vessel shall be required to depart and to put to sea within twenty-four hours after her entrance into such port, harbor, roadstead, or waters, except in case of stress of weather or of her requiring provisions or things necessary for the subsistence of her crew, or for repairs; in any of which cases the authorities of the port or of the nearest port (as the case may be) shall require her to put to sea as soon as possible after the expiration of such period of twenty-four hours, without permitting her to take in supplies beyond what may be necessary for her immediate use; and no such vessel which may have been permitted to remain within the waters of the United States for the purpose of repair shall continue within such port, harbor, roadstead, or waters for a longer period than twenty-four hours after her necessary repairs shall have been completed, unless within such twenty-four hours a vessel, whether ship of war, privateer, or merchant ship of an opposing belligerent, shall have departed therefrom, in which case the time limited for the departure of such ship of war or privateer shall be extended so far as may be necessary to secure an interval of not less than twenty-four hours between such departure and that of any ship of war, privateer, or merchant ship of an opposing belligerent which may have previously quit the same port, harbor, roadstead, or waters.

No ship of war or privateer of a belligerent shall be detained in any port, harbor, roadstead, or waters of the United States more than twenty-four hours, by reason of the successive departures from such port, harbor, roadstead, or waters of more than one vessel of an opposing belligerent. But if there be several vessels of opposing belligerents in the same port, harbor, roadstead, or waters, the order of their departure therefrom shall be so arranged as to afford the opportunity of leaving alternately to the vessels of the opposing belligerents, and to cause the least detention consistent with the objects of this proclamation.

No ship of war or privateer of a belligerent shall be permitted, while in any port, harbor, roadstead, or waters within the jurisdiction of the United States, to take in any supplies except provisions and such other things as may be requisite for the subsistence of her crew, and except so much coal only as may be sufficient to carry such vessel, if without any sail power, to the nearest port of her own country; or in case the vessel is rigged to go under sail, and may also be propelled by steam power, then with half the quantity of coal which she would be entitled to receive, if dependent upon steam alone, and no coal shall be again supplied to any such ship of war or privateer in the same or any other port, harbor, roadstead, or waters of the United States, without special permission, until after the expiration of three months from the time when such coal may have been last supplied to her within the waters of the United States, unless such ship of war or privateer shall, since last thus supplied, have entered a port of the government to which she belongs.

And I do further declare and proclaim that the statutes and the treaties of the United States and the law of nations alike require that no person, within the territory and jurisdiction of the United States, shall take part, directly or indirectly, in the said wars, but shall remain at peace with all of the said belligerents, and shall maintain a strict and impartial neutrality.

And I do hereby enjoin all citizens of the United States, and all persons residing or being within the territory or jurisdiction of the United States, to observe the laws thereof, and to commit no act contrary to the provisions of the said statutes or treaties or in violation of the law of nations in that behalf.

And I do hereby warn all citizens of the United States, and all persons residing or being within its territory or jurisdiction that, while the free and full expression of sympathies in public and private is not restricted by the laws of the United States, military forces in aid of a belligerent can not lawfully be originated or organized within its jurisdiction; and that, while all persons may lawfully and without restriction by reason of the aforesaid state of war manufacture and sell within the United States arms and munitions of war, and other articles ordinarily known as "contraband of war, yet they cannot carry such articles upon the high seas for the use or service of a belligerent, nor can they transport soldiers and officers of a belligerent, or attempt to break any blockade which may be lawfully established and maintained during the said wars without incurring the risk of hostile capture and the penalties denounced by the law of nations in that behalf.

And I do hereby give notice that all citizens of the United States and others who may claim the protection of this government, who may misconduct themselves in the premises, will do so at their peril, and that they can in no wise obtain any protection from the government of the United States against the consequences of their misconduct.

In Witness Whereof I have hereunto set my hand and caused the seal of the United States to be affixed.

Done at the city of Washington this fourth day of August in the year of our Lord one thousand nine hundred and fourteen and of the independence of the United States of America the one hundred and thirty-ninth.

WOODROW WILSON.

By the President:

WILLIAM JENNINGS BRYAN,
            Secretary of State.

APPENDIX 2

PRESIDENT WILSON'S STATEMENT
OF AUGUST 19, 1914[1]

My Fellow Countrymen: I suppose that every thoughtful man in America has asked himself, during these last troubled weeks, what influence the European war may exert upon the United States, and I take the liberty of addressing a few words to you in order to point out that it is entirely within our own choice what its effects upon us will be and to urge very earnestly upon you the sort of speech and conduct which will best safeguard the nation against distress and disaster.

The effect of the war upon the United States will depend upon what American citizens say and do. Every man who really loves America will act and speak in the true spirit of neutrality, which is the spirit of impartiality and fairness and friendliness to all concerned. The spirit of the nation in this critical matter will be determined largely by what individuals and society and those gathered in public meetings do and say, upon what newspapers and magazines contain, upon what ministers utter in their pulpits, and men proclaim as their opinions on the street.

The people of the United States are drawn from many nations, and chiefly from the nations now at war. It is natural and inevitable that there should be the utmost variety of sympathy and desire among them with regard to the issues and circumstances of the conflict. Some will wish one nation, others another, to succeed in the momentous struggle. It will be easy to excite passion and difficult to allay it. Those responsible for exciting it will assume a heavy responsibility, responsibility for no less a thing than that the people of the United States, whose love of their country and whose loyalty to its Government should unite them as Americans all, bound

[1]"Papers Relating to the Foreign Relations of the United States," 1914, Supplement, The World War, p. 551-2.

in honor and affection to think first of her and her interests, may be divided in camps of hostile opinion, hot against each other, involved in the war itself in impulse and opinion if not in action.

Such divisions among us would be fatal to our peace of mind and might seriously stand in the way of the proper performance of our duty as the one great nation at peace, the one people holding itself ready to play a part of impartial mediation and speak the counsels of peace and accommodation, not as a partisan, but as a friend.

I venture, therefore, my fellow countrymen, to speak a solemn word of warning to you against that deepest, most subtle, most essential breach of neutrality which may spring out of partisanship, out of passionately taking sides. The United States must be neutral in fact as well as in name during these days that are to try men's souls. We must be impartial in thought as well as in action, must put a curb upon our sentiments as well as upon every transaction that might be construed as a preference of one party to the struggle before another.

My thought is of America. I am speaking, I feel sure, the earnest wish and purpose of every thoughtful American that this great country of ours, which is, of course, the first in our thoughts and in our hearts, should show herself in this time of peculiar trial a nation fit beyond others to exhibit the fine poise of undisturbed judgment, the dignity of self-control, the efficiency of dispassionate action; a nation that neither sits in judgment upon others nor is disturbed in her own counsels and which keeps herself fit and free to do what is honest and disinterested and truly serviceable for the peace of the world.

Shall we not resolve to put upon ourselves the restraints which will bring to our people the happiness and the great and lasting influence for peace we covet for them?

WOODROW WILSON.

APPENDIX 3

THE ACT OF APRIL 13, 1934[1]
(*The So-Called "Johnson Act"*)

An Act to prohibit financial transactions with any foreign government in default on its obligations to the United States.

Be it enacted by the Senate and House of Representatives of the United States of America in Congress assembled, That hereafter it shall be unlawful within the United States or any place subject to the jurisdiction of the United States for any person to purchase or sell the bonds, securities, or other obligations of, any foreign government or political subdivision thereof or any organization or association acting for or on behalf of a foreign government or political subdivision thereof, issued after the passage of this Act, or to make any loan to such foreign government, political subdivision, organization, or association, except a renewal or adjustment of existing indebtedness while such government, political subdivision, organization, or association, is in default in the payment of its obligations, or any part thereof, to the Government of the United States. Any person violating the provisions of this Act shall upon conviction thereof be fined not more than $10,000 or imprisoned for not more than five years, or both.

SEC. 2. As used in this Act the term "person" includes individual, partnership, corporation, or association other than a public corporation created by or pursuant to special authorization of Congress, or a corporation in which the Government of the United States has or exercises a controlling interest through stock ownership or otherwise.

Approved, April 13, 1934.

[1]Public, No. 151, 73d Congress [S. 682]; 48 Statutes at Large 574.

166

APPENDIX 4

UNITED STATES NEUTRALITY LAWS, AS REVISED TO JANUARY 3, 1935[1]

CHAPTER 2.—OFFENSES AGAINST NEUTRALITY

Criminal Code, section 9

SECTION 21. *Accepting commission to serve against friendly power.* Every citizen of the United States who, within the territory or jurisdiction thereof, accepts and exercises a commission to serve a foreign prince, state, colony, district, or people, in war, by land or by sea, against any prince, state, colony, district, or people, with whom the United States are at peace, shall be fined not more than $2,000 and imprisoned not more than three years. (R. S. § 5281; Mar. 4, 1909, c. 321, § 9, 35 Stat. 1089.)

Criminal Code, section 10, amended

§ 22. *Enlisting in foreign service; exceptions.* Whoever, within the territory or jurisdiction of the United States, enlists or enters himself, or hires or retains another person to enlist or enter himself, or to go beyond the limits or jurisdiction of the United States with intent to be enlisted or entered in the service of any foreign prince, state, colony, district, or people as a soldier or as a marine or seaman on board of any vessel of war, letter of marque, or privateer shall be fined not more than $1,000 and imprisoned not more than three years: *Provided,* That this section shall not apply to citizens or subjects of any country engaged in war with a country with which the United States is at war, unless such citizen or subject of such foreign country shall hire or solicit a citizen of the United States to enlist or go beyond the jurisdiction of the United States with intent to enlist or enter the

[1]Chapter 2 of Title 18 of the Code of the Laws of the United States of America of a general and permanent character in force January 3, 1935. The provisions here printed embody the fundamental American legal rules concerning neutrality as they existed before they were supplemented by the neutrality legislation of 1935-1937. These basic provisions have not been changed since 1935.

service of a foreign country. Enlistments under this proviso shall be under regulations prescribed by the Secretary of War. (R. S. § 5282; Mar. 4, 1909, c. 321, § 10, 35 Stat. 1089; May 7, 1917, c. 11, 40 Stat. 39.)

Criminal Code, section 11

§ 23. *Arming vessels against friendly powers; forfeiture of vessel.* Whoever, within the territory or jurisdiction of the United States, fits out and arms, or attempts to fit out and arm, or procures to be fitted out and armed, or knowingly is concerned in the furnishing, fitting out, or arming of any vessel, with intent that such vessel shall be employed in the service of any foreign prince, or state, or of any colony, district, or people, to cruise, or commit hostilities against the subjects, citizens, or property of any foreign prince or state, or of any colony, district, or people, with whom the United States are at peace, or whoever issues or delivers a commission within the territory or jurisdiction of the United States for any vessel, to the intent that she may be so employed, shall be fined not more than $10,000 and imprisoned not more than three years. And every such vessel, her tackle, apparel, and furniture, together with all materials, arms, ammunition, and stores which may have been procured for the building and equipment thereof, shall be forfeited; one half to the use of the informer and the other half to the use of the United States. (R. S. § 5283; Mar. 4, 1909, c. 321, § 11, 35 Stat. 1090.)

Criminal Code, Section 12

§ 24. *Augmenting force of foreign armed vessel.* Whoever, within the territory or jurisdiction of the United States, increases or augments, or procures to be increased or augmented, or knowingly is concerned in increasing or augmenting, the force of any ship of war, cruiser, or other armed vessel which, at the time of her arrival within the United States, was a ship of war, or cruiser, or armed vessel, in the service of any foreign prince or state, or of any colony, district, or people, or belonging to the subjects or citizens of any such prince or state, colony, district, or people, the same being at war with any foreign prince or state, or of any colony, district, or people, with whom the United States are at peace, by adding to the number of the guns of such vessel, or by changing those on board of her for guns of a larger caliber, or by adding thereto any equipment solely applicable to war, shall be fined not more than $1,000 and imprisoned not more than one year.   (R. S. § 5285; Mar. 4, 1909, c. 321, § 12, 35 Stat. 1090.)

Criminal Code, section 13, amended

§ 25. *Organizing military expedition against friendly power.*   Whoever, within the territory or jurisdiction of the United States or of any of its possessions, knowingly begins or sets on foot or provides or prepares a means for or furnishes the money for, or who takes part in, any military or naval expedition or enterprise to be carried on from thence against the territory or dominion of any foreign prince or state, or of any colony, district, or people with whom the United States is at peace, shall be fined not more than $3,000 or imprisoned not more than three years, or both.   (R. S. § 5286; Mar. 4, 1909, c. 321, § 13, 35 Stat. 1090; June 15, 1917, c. 30, Title V, § 8, 40 Stat. 223.)

Criminal Code, section 14

§ 26. *Enforcement by courts; employment of land or naval forces.*   The district courts shall take cognizance of all complaints, by whomsoever instituted, in cases of captures made within the waters of the United States, or within a marine league of the coasts or shores thereof.   In every case in which a vessel is fitted out and armed, or attempted to be fitted out and armed, or in which the force of any vessel of war, cruiser, or other armed vessel is increased or augmented, or in which any military expedition or enterprise is begun or set on foot, contrary to the provisions and prohibitions of this chapter; and in every case of the capture of a vessel within the jurisdiction or protection of the United States as before defined; and in every case in which any process issuing out of any court of the United States is disobeyed or resisted by any person having the custody of any vessel of war, cruiser, or other armed vessel of any foreign prince or state, or of any colony, district, or people, or of any subjects or citizens of any foreign prince or state, or of any colony, district, or people, it shall be lawful for the President or such other person as he shall have empowered for that purpose, to employ such part of the land or naval forces of the United States, or of the militia thereof, for the purpose of taking possession of and detaining any such vessel, with her prizes, if any, in order to enforce the execution of the prohibitions and penalties of this chapter, and the restoring of such prizes in the cases in which restoration shall be adjudged; and also for the purpose of preventing the carrying on of any such expedition or enterprise from the territory or jurisdiction of the United States against the territory or dominion of any foreign prince or state, or of any colony, district, or people with whom the United States are at peace. (R. S. § 5287; Mar. 4, 1909, c. 321, § 14, 35 Stat. 1090.)

Criminal Code, section 15, amended

§ 27. *Compelling foreign vessels to depart.* It shall be lawful for the President to employ such part of the land or naval forces of the United States, or of the militia thereof, as he may deem necessary to compel any foreign vessel to depart from the United States or any of its possessions in all cases in which, by the law of nations or the treaties of the United States, it ought not to remain, and to detain or prevent any foreign vessel from so departing in all cases in which, by the law of nations or the treaties of the United States, it is not entitled to depart. (R. S. § 5288; Mar. 4, 1909, c. 321, § 15, 35 Stat. 1091; June 15, 1917, c. 30, Title V, § 10, 40 Stat. 223.)

Criminal Code, section 16

§ 28. *Bonds from armed vessels on clearing.* The owners or consignees of every armed vessel sailing out of the ports of, or under the jurisdiction of, the United States, belonging wholly or in part to citizens thereof, shall, before clearing out the same, give bond to the United States, with sufficient sureties, in double the amount of the value of the vessel and cargo on board, including her armament, conditioned that the vessel shall not be employed by such owners to cruise or commit hostilities against the subjects, citizens, or property of any foreign prince or state, or of any colony, district, or people with whom the United States are at peace. (R. S. § 5289; Mar. 4, 1909, c. 321, § 16, 35 Stat. 1091.)

Criminal Code, section 17

§ 29. *Detention by collectors of customs.* The several collectors of the customs shall detain any vessel manifestly built for warlike purposes, and about to depart the United States, or any place subject to the jurisdiction thereof, the cargo of which principally consists of arms and munitions of war, when the number of men shipped on board, or other circumstances, render it probable that such vessel is intended to be employed by the owners to cruise or commit hostilities upon the subjects, citizens, or property of any foreign prince or state, or of any colony, district, or people with whom the United States are at peace, until the decision of the President is had thereon, or until the owner gives such bond and security as is required of the owners of armed vessels by section 28 of this title. (R. S. § 5290; Mar. 4, 1909, c. 321, § 17, 35 Stat. 1091.)

Criminal Code, section 18

§ 30. *Construction of chapter; transient aliens; prosecutions for treason or piracy.* The provisions of sections 21 to 29 of this title shall not be construed to extend to any subject or citizen of any foreign prince, state, colony, district, or people who is transiently within the United States and enlists or enters himself on board of any vessel of war, letter of marque, or privateer, which at the time of its arrival within the United States was fitted and equipped as such, or hires or retains another subject or citizen of the same foreign prince, state, colony, district, or people who is transiently within the United States to enlist or enter himself to serve such foreign prince, state, colony, district, or people on board such vessel of war, letter of marque, or privateer, if the United States shall then be at peace with such foreign prince, state, colony, district, or people. Nor shall they be construed to prevent the prosecution or punishment of treason, or of any piracy defined by the laws of the United States. (R. S. § 5291; Mar. 4, 1909, c. 321, § 18, 35 Stat. 1091.)

§ 31. *Enforcement of neutrality; withholding clearance papers from vessels.* During a war in which the United States is a neutral nation, the President, or any person thereunto authorized by him, may withhold clearance from or to any vessel, domestic or foreign, which is required by law to secure clearance before departing from port or from the jurisdiction of the United States, or, by service of formal notice upon the owner, master, or person in command or having charge of any domestic vessel not required by law to secure clearances before so departing, to forbid its departure from port or from the jurisdiction of the United States, whenever there is reasonable cause to believe that any such vessel, domestic or foreign, whether requiring clearance or not, is about to carry fuel, arms, ammunition, men, supplies, dispatches, or information to any warship, tender, or supply ship of a foreign belligerent nation in violation of the laws, treaties, or obligations of the United States under the law of nations; and it shall thereupon be unlawful for such vessel to depart. (June 15, 1917, c. 30, Title V, § 1, 40 Stat. 221.)

§ 32. *Same; detention of armed vessels.* During a war in which the United States is a neutral nation, the President, or any person thereunto authorized by him, may detain any armed vessel owned wholly or in part by American citizens, or any vessel, domestic or foreign (other than one which has entered the ports of the United States as a public vessel), which is manifestly built for warlike purposes or has been converted or adapted from a private vessel to one suitable for warlike use, until the owner or master, or person having charge of such vessel, shall furnish proof satisfactory to the President, or to the person duly authorized by him, that the vessel will not be employed by the said owners, or master, or person having charge thereof, to cruise against or commit or attempt to commit hostilities upon the subjects, citizens, or property of any foreign prince or state, or of any colony, district, or people with which the United States is at peace, and that the said vessel will not be sold or delivered to any belligerent nation, or to an agent, officer, or citizen of such nation, by them or any of them, within the jurisdiction of the United States, or, having left that jurisdiction, upon the high seas. (June 15, 1917, c. 30, Title V, § 2, 40 Stat. 221.)

§ 33. *Same; sending out armed vessel with intent to deliver to belligerent nation.* During a war in which the United States is a neutral nation, it shall be unlawful to send out of the jurisdiction of the United States any vessel built, armed, or equipped as a vessel of war, or converted from a private vessel into a vessel of war, with any intent or under any agreement or contract, written or oral, that such vessel shall be delivered to a belligerent nation, or to an agent, officer, or citizen of such nation, or with reasonable cause to believe that the said vessel shall or will be employed in the service of any such belligerent nation after its departure from the jurisdiction of the United States. (June 15, 1917, c. 30, Title V, § 3, 40 Stat. 222.)

§ 34. *Same; statement from master that cargo will not be delivered to other vessels.* During a war in which the United States is a neutral nation, in addition to the facts

required by sections 91, 92, and 94 of Title 46 to be set out
in the masters' and shippers' manifests before clearance will
be issued to vessels bound to foreign ports, each of which
sections is hereby declared to be and is continued in full force
and effect, every master or person having charge or command of any vessel, domestic or foreign, whether requiring
clearance or not, before departure of such vessel from port
shall deliver to the collector of customs for the district
wherein such vessel is then located a statement, duly verified
by oath, that the cargo or any part of the cargo is or is not
to be delivered to other vessels in port or to be transshipped
on the high seas, and, if it is to be so delivered or transshipped, stating the kind and quantities and the value of the
total quantity of each kind of article so to be delivered or
transshipped, and the name of the person, corporation, vessel,
or government to whom the delivery or transshipment is to
be made; and the owners, shippers, or consignors of the
cargo of such vessel shall in the same manner and under the
same conditions deliver to the collector like statements under
oath as to the cargo or the parts thereof laden or shipped
by them, respectively. (June 15, 1917, c. 30, Title V, § 4, 40
Stat. 222.)

§ 35. *Same; forbidding departure of vessels.* Whenever
it appears that the vessel is not entitled to clearance or whenever there is reasonable cause to believe that the additional
statements under oath required in section 34 of this title are
false, the collector of customs for the district in which the
vessel is located may, subject to review by the Secretary of
Commerce, refuse clearance to any vessel, domestic or foreign, and by formal notice served upon the owners, master,
or person or persons in command or charge of any domestic
vessel for which clearance is not required by law, forbid the
departure of the vessel from the port or from the jurisdiction
of the United States; and it shall thereupon be unlawful for
the vessel to depart. (June 15, 1917, c. 30, Title V, § 5,
40 Stat. 222.)

§ 36. *Same; unlawful taking of vessel out of port.* Whoever, in violation of any of the provisions of sections 25, 27, and 31 to 38 of this title, shall take, or attempt or conspire to take, or authorize the taking of any such vessel, out of port or from the jurisdiction of the United States, shall be fined not more than $10,000 or imprisoned not more than five years, or both; and, in addition, such vessel, her tackle, apparel, furniture, equipment, and her cargo shall be forfeited to the United States. (June 15, 1917, c. 30, Title V, § 6, 40 Stat. 222.)

§ 37. *Same; internment of person belonging to armed land or naval forces of belligerent nation; arrest; punishment for aiding escape.* Whoever, being a person belonging to the armed land or naval forces of a belligerent nation or belligerent faction of any nation and being interned in the United States, in accordance with the law of nations, shall leave or attempt to leave said jurisdiction, or shall leave or attempt to leave the limits of internment in which freedom of movement has been allowed, without permission from the proper official of the United States in charge, or shall willfully overstay a leave of absence granted by such official, shall be subject to arrest by any marshal or deputy marshal of the United States, or by the military or naval authorities thereof, and shall be returned to the place of internment and there confined and safely kept for such period of time as the official of the United States in charge shall direct; and whoever, within the jurisdiction of the United States and subject thereto, shall aid or entice any interned person to escape or attempt to escape from the jurisdiction of the United States, or from the limits of internment prescribed, shall be fined not more than $1,000 or imprisoned not more than one year, or both. (June 15, 1917, c. 30, Title V, § 7, 40 Stat. 223.)

§ 38. *Same; enforcement of sections 25, 27, and 31 to 37 of this title.* The President may employ such part of the land or naval forces of the United States as he may deem necessary to carry out the purposes of sections 25, 27, and

31 to 37 of this title.   (June 15, 1917, c. 30, Title V, § 9, 40 Stat. 223.)

§ 39. *Same; United States defined; jurisdiction of offenses; prior offenses; partial invalidity of provisions.* The term "United States", as used in sections 25, 27, and 31 to 38 of this title, includes the Canal Zone, and all territory and waters, continental or insular, subject to the jurisdiction of the United States. The several courts of first instance in the Philippine Islands and the district court of the Canal Zone shall have jurisdiction of offenses under said sections 25, 27, and 31 to 38 committed within their respective districts, and concurrent jurisdiction with the district courts of the United States of offenses thereunder committed upon the high seas, and of conspiracies to commit such offenses, as defined by section 88 of this title, and the provisions of said section 88, for the purposes of sections 25, 27, and 31 to 38 of this title, are extended to the Philippine Islands and to the Canal Zone. Offenses committed and penalties, forfeitures, or liabilities incurred prior to June 15, 1917, under any law embraced in or changed, modified, or repealed by sections 25, 27, and 31 to 38 may be prosecuted and punished, and suits and proceedings for causes arising or acts done or committed prior to June 15, 1917, may be commenced and prosecuted, in the same manner and with the same effect as if said sections 25, 27, and 31 to 38 had not been passed. If any clause, sentence, paragraph, or part of sections 25, 27, and 31 to 38 shall for any reason be adjudged by any court of competent jurisdiction to be invalid, such judgment shall not affect, impair, or invalidate the remainder thereof but shall be confined in its operation to the clause, sentence, paragraph, or part thereof directly involved in the controversy in which such judgment shall have been rendered. (June 15, 1917, c. 30, Title XIII, §§ 1 to 4, 40 Stat. 231.)

APPENDIX 5

NEUTRALITY ACT OF MAY 1, 1937[1]

That the joint resolution entitled Joint resolution providing for the prohibition of the export of arms, ammunition and implements of war to belligerent countries; the prohibition of the transportation of arms, ammunition and implements of war by vessels of the United States for the use of belligerent States; for the registration and licensing of persons engaged in the business of manufacturing, exporting or importing arms, ammunition or implements of war; and restricting travel by American citizens on belligerent ships during war," approved August 31, 1935, as amended, is amended to read as follows:

Export of Arms, Ammunition, and Implements of War

Section 1

(a) Whenever the President shall find that there exists a state of war between, or among, two or more foreign states, the President shall proclaim such fact, and it shall thereafter be unlawful to export, or attempt to export, or cause to be exported, arms, ammunition, or implements of war from any place in the United States to any belligerent state named in such proclamation, or to any neutral state for transshipment to, or for the use of, any such belligerent state.

(b) The President shall, from time to time, by proclamation, extend such embargo upon the export of arms, ammunition, or implements of war to other states as and when they may become involved in such war.

(c) Whenever the President shall find that a state of civil strife exists in a foreign state and that such civil strife is of a magnitude or is being conducted under such conditions that the export of arms, ammunitions, or implements of war

[1]Public Resolution, No. 27, 75th Congress [S. J. Res. 51].

177

from the United States to such foreign state would threaten or endanger the peace of the United States, the President shall proclaim such fact, and it shall thereafter be unlawful to export, or attempt to export, or cause to be exported, arms, ammunition, or implements of war from any place in the United States to such foreign state, or to any neutral State for transshipment to, or for the use of, such foreign State.

(d) The President shall, from time to time, by proclamation, definitely enumerate the arms, ammunition, and implements of war, the export of which is prohibited by this section. The arms, ammunition, and implements of war so enumerated shall include those enumerated in the President's proclamation Numbered 2163, of April 10, 1936, but shall not include raw materials or any other articles or materials not of the same general character as those enumerated in the said proclamation, and in the Convention for the Supervision of the International Trade in Arms and Ammunition and in Implements of War, signed at Geneva June 17, 1925.

(e) Whoever, in violation of any of the provisions of this act, shall export, or attempt to export, or cause to be exported, arms, ammunition, or implements of war from the United States shall be fined not more than $10,000, or imprisoned not more than five years, or both, and the property, vessel, or vehicle containing the same shall be subject to the provisions of sections 1 to 8, inclusive, title 6, chapter 30, of the Act approved June 15, 1917 (40 Stat. 223-225; U. S. C., 1934 ed., title 22, secs. 238-245).

(f) In the case of the forefiture of any arms, ammunitions, or implements of war by reason of a violation of this Act, no public or private sale shall be required; but such arms, ammunition, or implements of war shall be delivered to the Secretary of War for such use or disposal thereof as shall be approved by the President of the United States.

(g) Whenever, in the judgment of the President, the conditions which have caused him to issue any proclamation under the authority of this section have ceased to exist, he shall revoke the same, and the provisions of this section shall thereupon cease to apply with respect to the state or states named in such proclamation, except with respect to offenses committed, or forfeitures incurred, prior to such revocation.

EXPORT OF OTHER ARTICLES AND MATERIALS[2]

Section 2

(a) Whenever the President shall have issued a proclamation under the authority of section 1 of this Act and he shall thereafter find that the placing of restrictions on the shipment of certain articles or materials in addition to arms, ammunition, and implements of war from the United States to belligerent states, or to a state wherein civil strife exists, is necessary to promote the security or preserve the peace of the United States or to protect the lives of citizens of the United States, he shall so proclaim, and it shall thereafter be unlawful, except under such limitations and exceptions as the President may prescribe as to lakes, rivers, and inland waters bordering on the United States, and as to transportation on or over lands bordering on the United States, for any American vessel to carry such articles or materials to any belligerent state, or any state wherein civil strife exists, named in such proclamation issued under the authority of section 1 of this Act, or to any neutral state for transshipment to, or for the use of, any such belligerent state or any such state wherein civil strife exists.

The President shall by proclamation from time to time definitely enumerate the articles and materials which it shall be unlawful for American vessels to so transport.

[2]This section of the Act, generally known as the "cash-and-carry" provision, expired by limitation on May 1, 1939.

(b) Whenever the President shall have issued a proclamation under the authority of section 1 of this Act and he shall thereafter find that the placing of restrictions on the export of articles or materials from the United States to belligerent states, or to a state wherein civil strife exists, is necessary to promote the security or preserve the peace of the United States or to protect the lives or commerce of citizens of the United States, he shall so proclaim, and it shall thereafter be unlawful, except under such limitations and exceptions as the President may prescribe as to lakes, rivers, and inland waters bordering on the United States, and as to transportation on or over lands bordering on the United States, to export or transport, or attempt to export or transport, or cause to be exported or transported from the United States to any belligerent state, or to any state wherein civil strife exists, named in such proclamation issued under the authority of section 1 of this Act, or to any neutral state for transshipment to, or for the use of, any such belligerent state, or any such state wherein civil strife exists, any articles or materials whatever until all right, title, and interest therein shall have been transferred to some foreign government, agency, institution, association, partnership, corporation, or national.

The shipper of such articles or materials shall be required to file with the collector of the port from which they are to be exported a declaration under oath that there exists in citizens of the United States no right, title, or interest in such articles or materials, and to comply with such rules and regulations as shall be promulgated from time to time by the President. Any such declaration so filed shall be a conclusive estoppel against any claim of any citizen of the United States of right, title, or interest in such articles or materials.

Insurance written by underwriters on any articles or materials the export of which is prohibited by this Act, or on articles or materials carried by an American vessel in violation of subsection (a) of this section, shall not be deemed an American interest therein, and no insurance policy issued on such articles or materials and no loss incurred thereunder or by the owner of the vessel carrying the same shall be made a basis of any claim put forward by the Government of the United States.

(c) The President shall from time to time by proclamation extend such restrictions as are imposed under the authority of this section to other states as and when they may be declared to become belligerent states under proclamations issued under the authority of section 1 of this Act.

(d) The President may from time to time change, modify or revoke in whole or in part any proclamations issued by him under the authority of this section.

(e) Except with respect to offenses committed, or forfeitures incurred, prior to May 1, 1939, this section and all proclamations issued thereunder shall not be effective after May 1, 1939.

FINANCIAL TRANSACTIONS

Section 3

(a) Whenever the President shall have issued a proclamation under the authority of section 1 of this Act, it shall thereafter be unlawful for any person within the United States to purchase, sell, or exchange bonds, securities, or other obligations of the government of any belligerent state or of any state wherein civil strife exists, named in such proclamation, or of any political subdivision of any such state, or of any person acting for or on behalf of the government of any such state, or of any faction or asserted government within any such state wherein civil strife exists, or of any person acting for or on behalf of any faction or asserted government within any such state wherein civil strife exists, issued after the date of such proclamation, or to make any loan or extend any credit to any such government, political subdivision faction, asserted government, or person, or to solicit or receive any contribution for any such government, political subdivision, faction, asserted government, or person: Provided, that if the President shall find that such action will serve to protect the commercial or other interests of the United States or its citizens, he may, in his discretion, and to such extent and under such regulations as he may prescribe, except from the operation of this section ordinary commercial credits and short-time obligations in aid of legal transactions and of a character customarily used in normal peacetime commercial transactions.

Nothing in this subsection shall be construed to prohibit the solicitation or collection of funds to be used for medical aid and assistance, or for food and clothing to relieve human suffering, when such solicitation or collection of funds is made on behalf of and for use by any person or organization which is not acting for or on behalf of any such government, political subdivision, faction, or asserted government, but all such solicitations and collections of funds shall be subject to the approval of the President and shall be made under such rules and regulations as he shall prescribe.

(b) The provisions of this section shall not apply to a renewal or adjustment of such indebtedness as may exist on the date of the President's proclamation.

(c) Whoever shall violate the provisions of this section or of any regulations issued hereunder shall, upon conviction thereof, be fined not more than $50,000 or imprisoned for not more than five years, or both. Should the violation be by a corporation, organization, or association, each officer or agent thereof participating in the violation may be liable to the penalty herein prescribed.

(d) Whenever the President shall have revoked any such proclamation issued under the authority of section 1 of this Act, the provisions of this section and of any regulations issued by the President hereunder shall thereupon cease to apply with respect to the state or states named in such proclamation, except with respect to offenses committed prior to such revocation.

EXCEPTIONS—AMERICAN REPUBLICS

Section 4

This act shall not apply to an American republic or republics engaged in war against a non-American state or states, provided the American republic is not cooperating with a non-American state or states in such war.

NATIONAL MUNITIONS CONTROL BOARD

Section 5

(a) There is hereby established a National Munitions Control Board (hereinafter referred to as the "Board") to carry out the provisions of this act. The board shall consist of the Secretary of State, who shall be chairman and executive officer of the Board, the Secretary of the Treasury, the Secretary of War, the Secretary of the Navy, and the Secretary of Commerce.

Except as otherwise provided in this Act, or by other law, the administration of this Act is vested in the Department of State. The Secretary of State shall promulgate such rules and regulations with regard to the enforcement of this section as he may deem necessary to carry out its provisions.

The Board shall be convened by the chairman and shall hold at least one meeting a year.

(b) Every person who engages in the business of manufacturing, exporting, or importing any of the arms, ammunition, or implements of war referred to in this Act, whether as an exporter, importer, manufacturer, or dealer, shall register with the Secretary of State his name, or business name, principal place of business, and places of business in the United States, and a list of the arms, ammunition, and implements of war which he manufactures, imports, or exports.

(c) Every person required to register under this section shall notify the Secretary of State of any change in the arms, ammunition, or implements of war which he exports, imports, or manufactures; and upon such notification the Secretary of State shall issue to such person an amended certificate of registration, free of charge, which shall remain valid until the date of expiration of the original certificate. Every person required to register under the provisions of this section shall pay a registration fee of $500, unless he manufactured, exported, or imported arms, ammunition, and implements of war to a total sales value of less than $50,000 during the twelve months immediately preceding his registration, in which case he shall pay a registration fee of $100.

Upon receipt of the required registration fee, the Secretary of State shall issue a registration certificate valid for five years, which shall be renewable for further periods of five years upon the payment for each renewal of a fee of $500 in the case of persons who manufactured, exported, or imported arms, ammunition, and implements of war to a total sales value of more than $50,000 during the twelve months immediately preceding the renewal, or a fee of $100 in the case of persons who manufactured, exported, or imported arms, ammunition, and implements of war to a total sales value of less than $50,000 during the twelve months immediately preceding the renewal.

The Secretary of the Treasury is hereby directed to refund, out of any moneys in the Treasury not otherwise appropriated, the sum of $400 to every person who shall have paid a registration fee of $500 pursuant to this act, who manufactured, exported, or imported arms, ammunition, and implements of war to a total sales value of less than $50,000 during the twelve months immediately preceding his registration.

(d) It shall be unlawful for any person to export, or attempt to export, from the United States to any other state, any of the arms, ammunition, or implements of war referred to in this Act, or to import, or attempt to import, to the United States from any other state, any of the arms, ammunition, or implements of war referred to in this Act, without first having obtained a license therefor.

(e) All persons required to register under this section shall maintain, subject to the inspection of the Secretary of State, or any person or persons designated by him, such permanent records of manufacture for export, importation, and exportation of arms, ammunition, and implements of war as the Secretary of State shall prescribe.

(f) Licenses shall be issued to persons who have registered as herein provided for, except in cases of export or import licenses where the export of arms, ammunition, or implements of war would be in violation of this Act or any other law of the United States, or of a treaty to which the United States is a party, in which cases such licenses shall not be issued.

(g) Whenever the President shall have issued a proclamation under the authority of section 1 of this Act, all licenses theretofore issued under this act shall be ipso facto and immediately upon the issuance of such proclamation, cease to grant authority to export arms, ammunition, or implements of war from any place in the United States to any belligerent state, or to any state wherein civil strife exists, named in such proclamation, or to any neutral state for transshipment to, or for the use of, any such belligerent state or any such state wherein civil strife exists; and said licenses, in so far as the grant of authority to export to the state or states named in such proclamation is concerned, shall be null and void.

(h) No purchase of arms, ammunition, or implements of war shall be made on behalf of the United States by any officer, executive department, or independent establishment of the Government from any person who shall have failed to register under the provisions of this Act.

(i) The provisions of the Act of August 29, 1916, relating to the sale of ordinance and stores to the Government of

Cuba (39 Stat. 619, 643; U. S. C., 1934 ed., title 50, sec. 72), are hereby repealed as of Dec. 31, 1937.

(j) The Board shall make an annual report to Congress, copies of which shall be distributed as are other reports transmitted to Congress. Such reports shall contain such information and data collected by the Board as may be considered of value in the determination of questions connected with the control of trade in arms, ammunition, and implements of war. The board shall include in such reports a list of all persons required to register under the provisions of this Act, and full information concerning the licenses issued hereunder.

(k) The President is hereby authorized to proclaim upon recommendation of the Board from time to time a list of articles which shall be considered arms, ammunition, and implements of war for the purposes of this section.

American Vessels Prohibited From Carrying Arms to Belligerent States

Section 6

(a) Whenever the President shall have issued a proclamation under the authority of section 1 of this Act, it shall thereafter be unlawful, until such proclamation is revoked, for any American vessel to carry any arms, ammunition or implements of war to any belligerent state, or to any state wherein civil strife exists, named in such proclamation, or to any neutral state for transshipment to, or for the use of, any such belligerent state or any such state wherein civil strife exists.

(b) Whoever, in violation of the provisions of this section, shall take, or attempt to take, or shall authorize, hire or solicit another to take, any American vessel carrying such cargo out of port or from the jurisdiction of the United States shall be fined not more than $10,000, or imprisoned not more than five years, or both; and, in addition such vessel, and her tackle, apparel, furniture, and equipment, and the arms, ammunition, and implements of war on board, shall be forfeited to the United States.

Use of American Ports As Base of Supply

Section 7

(a) Whenever, during any war in which the United States is neutral, the President, or any person thereunto authorized by him, shall have cause to believe that any vessel, domestic or foreign, whether requiring clearance or not, is about to carry out of a port of the United States, fuel, men, arms, ammunition, implements of war, or other supplies to any warship, tender, or supply ship of a belligerent state, but the evidence is not deemed sufficient to justify forbidding the departure of the vessel as provided by section 1, title V, chapter 30, of the Act approved June 15, 1917 (40 Stat. 217, 221; U. S. C., 1934 ed., title 18, sec. 31), and if, in the President's judgment, such action will serve to maintain peace between the United States and foreign states, or to protect the commercial interests of the United States and its citizens, or to promote the security or neutrality of the United States, he shall have the power and it shall be his duty to require the owner, master, or person in command thereof, before departing from a port of the United States, to give a bond to the United States, with sufficient sureties, in such amount as he shall deem proper, conditioned that the vessel will not deliver the men, or any part of the cargo, to any warship, tender, or supply ship of a belligerent state.

(b) If the President, or any person thereunto authorized by him, shall find that a vessel, domestic or foreign, in a port of the United States, has previously cleared from a port of the United States during such war and delivered its cargo or any part thereof to a warship, tender, or supply ship of a belligerent state, he may prohibit the departure of such vessel during the duration of the war.

SUBMARINES AND ARMED MERCHANT VESSELS

Section 8

Whenever, during any war in which the United States is neutral, the President shall find that special restrictions placed on the use of the ports and territorial waters of the United States by the submarines or armed merchant vessels of a foreign state, will serve to maintain peace between the United States and foreign states, or to protect the commercial interests of the United States and its citizens, or to promote the security of the United States, and shall make proclamation thereof, it shall thereafter be unlawful for any such submarine or armed merchant vessel to enter a port or the territorial waters of the United States or to depart therefrom, except under such conditions and subject to such limitations as the President may prescribe. Whenever, in his judgment, the conditions which have caused him to issue such proclamation have ceased to exist, he shall revoke his proclamation and the provisions of this section shall thereupon cease to apply.

TRAVEL ON VESSELS OF BELLIGERENT STATES

Section 9

Whenever the President shall have issued a proclamation under the authority of section 1 of this Act, it shall thereafter be unlawful for any citizen of the United States to travel on any vessel of the state or states named in such proclamation, except in accordance with such rules and regulations as the President shall prescribe: Provided, however, that the provisions of the this section shall not apply to a citizen of the United States traveling on a vessel whose voyage was begun in advance of the date of the President's proclamation and who had no opportunity to discontinue his voyage after that date: And provided further, that they shall not apply under ninety days after the date of the President's proclamation to a citizen of the United States returning from a foreign state to the United States.

Whenever, in the President's judgment, the conditions which have caused him to issue his proclamation have ceased to exist, he shall revoke his proclamation, and the provisions of this section shall thereupon cease to apply with respect to the state or states named in such proclamation, except with respect to offenses committed prior to such revocation.

ARMING OF AMERICAN MERCHANT VESSELS PROHIBITED

Section 10

Whenever the President shall have issued a proclamation under the authority of section 1, it shall thereafter be unlawful, until such proclamation is revoked, for any American vessel engaged in commerce with any belligerent state, or any state wherein civil strife exists, named in such proclamation, to be armed or to carry any armament, arms, ammunition, or implements of war, except small arms and ammunition therefor which the President may deem necessary and shall publicly designate for the preservation of discipline aboard such vessels.

REGULATIONS

Section 11

The President may, from time to time, promulgate such rules and regulations, not inconsistent with law, as may be necessary and proper to carry out any of the provisions of this Act; and he may exercise any power or authority conferred on him by this Act through such officer or officers, or agency or agencies, as he shall direct.

GENERAL PENALTY PROVISION

Section 12

In every case of the violation of any of the provisions of this Act or of any rule or regulation issued pursuant thereto where a specific penalty is not herein provided, such violator or violators, upon conviction, shall be fined not more than $10,000, or imprisoned not more than five years, or both.

DEFINITIONS

Section 13

For the purpose of this Act—

(a) The term "United States," when used in a geographical sense, includes the several States and Territories, the insular possessions of the United States (including the Philippine Islands), the Canal Zone, and the District of Columbia.

(b) The term "person" includes a partnership, company, association, or corporation, as well as a natural person.

(c) The term "vessel" means every description of watercraft (including aircraft) or other contrivance used, or capable of being used, as a means of transportation on, under, or over water.

(d) The term "American vessel" means any vessel (including aircraft) documented under the laws of the United States.

(e) The term "vehicle" means every description of carriage (including aircraft) or other contrivance used, or capable of being used, as a means of transportation on or over land.

(f) The term "state" shall include nation, government, and country.

SEPARABILITY OF PROVISIONS

Section 14

If any of the provisions of this Act, or the application thereof to any person or circumstance, is held invalid, the remainder of the Act, and the application of such provision to other persons or circumstances, shall not be affected thereby.

APPROPRIATIONS

Section 15

There is hereby authorized to be appropriated from time to time, out of any money in the Treasury not otherwise appropriated, such amounts as may be necessary to carry out the provisions and accomplish the purposes of this Act.

APPENDIX 6

PRESIDENT ROOSEVELT'S MESSAGE OF JULY 14, 1939, WITH SECRETARY HULL'S STATEMENT CONCERNING NEUTRALITY LEGISLATION[1]

To the Congress of the United States:

I am advised that by a vote of twelve to eleven the Senate Committee on Foreign Relations has deferred action on peace and neutrality legislation until the next session of the Congress.

I am appending hereto a statement from the Secretary of State which has my full approval, and which I trust will receive your earnest attention.

It has been abundantly clear to me for some time that for the cause of peace and in the interests of American neutrality and security it is highly advisable that the Congress at this session should take certain much needed action. In the light of present world conditions I see no reason to change that opinion.

FRANKLIN D. ROOSEVELT.

HULL'S STATEMENT

The statement by Secretary Hull transmitted by President Roosevelt to Congress read:

The cornerstone of the foreign policy of the United States is the preservation of the peace and security of our nation, the strengthening of international law, and the revitalization of international good faith. The foreign policy of this government may be misinterpreted or it may be misunderstood, but it cannot be destroyed. Peace is so precious and war so devastating that the people of the United States and their government must not fail to make their just and legitimate contribution to the preservation of peace.

[1]Department of State Press Release.

The Congress has pending before it at the present time certain proposals providing for the amendment of the existing so-called neutrality legislation. Some of these proposed changes I regard as necessary to promote the peace and security of the United States.

There is an astonishing amount of confusion and misunderstanding as regards the legislation under consideration, and particularly with regard to the operation of the existing arms embargo.

I shall try to bring out as clearly as I can the important points of agreement and disagreement between those who support the principles contained in the six point peace and neutrality program recommended by the Executive branch of the Government and those who oppose these recommendations.

In substance and in principle both sides of the discussion agree on the following points:

1. Both sides agree that the first concern of the United States must be its own peace and security.

2. Both sides agree that it should be the policy of this government to avoid being drawn into wars between other nations.

3. Both sides agree that this nation should at all times avoid entangling alliances or involvements with other nations.

4. Both sides agree that in the event of foreign wars this nation should maintain a status of strict neutrality, and that around the structure of neutrality we should so shape our policies as to keep this country from being drawn into war.

On the other hand, the following is the chief essential point of disagreement between those who favor the adoption of the recommendations formulated by the Executive branch of the Government and those who are opposing these recommendations:

The proponents, including the Executive branch of the Government, at the time when the arms embargo was originally adopted called attention to the fact that its enactment constitued a hazardous departure from the principle of international law which recognizes the right of neutrals to trade with belligerents and of belligerents to trade with neutrals.

They believe that neutrality means impartiality, and, in their view an arms embargo is directly opposed to the idea of neutrality. It is not humanly possible, by enacting an arms embargo, or by refraining from such enactment, to hold the scales exactly even between two belligerents. In either case and due to shifting circumstances one belligerent may find itself in a position of relative advantage or disadvantage.

The important difference between the two cases is that when such a condition arises in the absence of an arms embargo on our part, no responsibility attaches to this country, whereas in the presence of an embargo, the responsibility of this country for the creation of the condition is inevitably direct and clear.

There is no theory or practice to be found in international law pertaining to neutrality to the effect that the advantages that any particular belligerent might procure through its geographic location, its superiority on land or at sea, or through other circumstances, should be offset by the establishment by neutral nations of embargoes.

The opposition to the present substitute proposal joins issue on this point and stands for existing rigid embargo as a permanent part of our neutrality policy.

And yet by insisting on an arms embargo in time of war they are, to that extent, for the reasons I have stated, urging not neutrality but what might well result in actual unneutrality, the serious consequences of which no one can predict.

Those who urge the retention of the present embargo continue to advance the view that it will keep this country out of war—thereby misleading the American people to rely upon a false and illogical delusion as a means of keeping out of war.

I say it is illogical, because, while the trade in "arms, ammunition and implements of war" is at present banned, the trade in equally essential war materials, as well as all the essential materials out of which the finished articles are made, can continue.

For example, in time of war, we can sell cotton for the manufacture of explosives but not the explosives; we can sell the steel and copper for cannon and for shells, but not the cannon nor the shells; we can continue to sell to belligerents the high-powered fuel necessary for the operation of airplanes, but we are not able to sell the airplanes.

I say it is a false delusion because a continuation of the trade in arms is a clearly recognized and traditional right of the nationals of a neutral country in time of war, subject only to effective blockade and to the right of belligerents to treat any such commodities as contraband.

The assertion frequently made that this country has ever engaged or may become engaged in serious controversy solely over the fact that its nationals have sold arms to belligerents is misleading and unsupportable.

All available evidence is directly to the contrary. Every informed person knows that arms, as absolute contraband, are subject to seisure by the belligerent and that neither the neutral shipper nor his government has the slightest ground for complaint.

There is, therefore, no reason to suppose that the sale of arms may lead to serious controversy between a neutral and a belligerent. Furthermore, under the proposals that have been made American nationals would be divested of all right, title and interest in these and other commodities before they leave our shores and American citizens and ships would be kept out of the danger zones.

As regards possible complications which might arise as a result of the extension of credits to belligerents or of extraordinary profits accruing to any group of producers in this country, it is wholly within the power of Congress at all times to safeguard the national interest in this respect.

Controversies which would involve the United States are far more likely to arise from the entrance of American ships or American citizens in the danger zones or through the sinking on the high seas of American vessels carrying commodities other than those covered by the arms embargo.

In the recommendations formulated by the Executive as a substitute for the present legislation it was especially urged that provisions be adopted which would exclude American nationals and American ships from zones where real danger to their safety might exist and which would divest goods of American ownership, thereby minimizing to the fullest extent the danger of American involvement.

Those of us who support the recommendations formulated for the elimination of the embargo are convinced that the arms embargo plays into the hands of those nations which have taken the lead in building up their fighting power.

It works directly against the interests of the peace-loving nations, especially those which do not possess their own munitions plants.

It means that if any country is disposed toward conquest and devotes its energy and resources to establish itself as a superior fighting power, that country may be more tempted to try the fortunes of war if it knows that its less well prepared opponents would be shut off from those supplies which, under every rule of international law, they should be able to buy in all neutral countries, including the United States.

It means also that some of those countries which have only limited facilities for the production of arms, ammunition and implements of war, are put in a position of increased dependence. During peace-time they would feel the compulsion of shaping their political as well as their economic policy to suit the military strength of others, and during wartime their powers of defense would be limited.

For these reasons those who are supporting the recommendations for the amendment of existing legislation recognize definitely that the present embargo encourages a general state of war both in Europe and Asia. Since the present embargo has this effect its results are directly prejudicial to the highest interests and to the peace and to the security of the United States.

In the present grave conditions of international anarchy and of danger to peace, in more than one part of the world, I profoundly believe that the first great step toward safeguarding this nation from being drawn into war is to use whatever influence it can, compatible with the traditional policy of our country of non-involvement, so as to make less likely the outbreak of a major war.

This is a duty placed upon our government which some may fail to perceive or choose to reject. But it must be clear to every one of us that the outbreak of a general war increases the dangers confronting the United States. This fact cannot be ignored.

I would emphasize that the course proposed through the substitute legislation recommended by the Executive is consistent with the rules of international law and with the policy of our own country over a period of 150 years.

The basis for the recommendations made is the firm intention of keeping this country from being drawn into war. If there existed any desire to assist or to injure particular foreign countries this government would not have been endeavoring persistently, within the limitations of our traditional policy over a period of many years, to do its utmost to avoid the outbreak of a general war.

I earnestly hope that the Congress will lend the fullest measure of its cooperation in the endeavor to avoid war in the first place and to place this country in a position of the greatest security possible, should war break out. In the tragic event that peace efforts fail and that a major war occurs, there will be general agreement within the United States that every effort must be exerted to keep this country from being drawn therein.

I must also refer to the impression sedulously created to the effect that the sale of arms, munitions and implements of war by this country is immoral and that on this ground it should be suppressed in time of war.

As a matter of fact, almost all sales of arms and ammunition made in recent years by our nationals have been made to governments whose policies have been dedicated to the maintenance of peace, but who have felt the necessity of creating or of augmenting their means of national self-defense, thereby protecting otherwise helpless men, women and children in the event that other powers resort to war.

In the face of the present universal danger, all countries, including our own, feel the necessity of increasing armament, and small countries in particular are dependent upon countries like the United States, which have the capacity to produce armaments.

Our refusal to make it possible for them to obtain such means of necessary self-defense in a time of grave emergency would contribute solely towards making more helpless the law-abiding and peace-devoted peoples of the world.

If such action is moral, and if, on the contrary, sales of the means of self-defense for the protection of peaceful and law-abiding peoples are immoral, then a new definition of morality and immorality must be written. This task might be left to the proponents of the arms embargo.

I must also refer to another impression created by propaganda to the effect that the abandonment of the arms embargo would increase power of action on the part of the executive branch of the government and conversely that the maintenance of the embargo would serve as an additional check on the powers of the executive.

It is difficult to see how either of these propositions could possibly hold true. An impartial granting of access to American markets to all countries without distinction gives the executive no additional power to choose among them and to commit this country to any line of policy or action which may lead it either into a dangerous controversy or into war with any foreign power.

The legislative proposals which were recommended to the Congress through the communications which I transmitted to Senator Pittman and to Congressman Bloom on May 27 providing for the safe-guarding of our nation to the fullest possible extent from incurring the risks of involvement in war contemplate the elimination of the existing arms embargo and are as follows:

(1) To prohibit American ships from entering combat areas;

(2) To restrict travel by American citizens in combat areas;

(3) To require that goods exported from the United States to belligerent countries shall be preceded by the transfer of title to the foreign purchasers;

(4) To continue the existing legislation respecting loans and credits to belligerent nations;

(5) To regulate the solicitation and collection in this country of funds for belligerents; and

(6) To continue the national munitions control board and the licensing system with respect to the importation and exportation of arms, and implements of war.

This six-point program was the best that could be devised after much painstaking thought and study, and after many conferences with members of the Congress, of how best to keep this country out of a conflict should it arise.

It rests primarily on the established rules of international law, plus the curtailment of certain rights of our nationals, the exercise of which is permitted under international law but which might lead to controversies with belligerents and eventual involvement in foreign wars.

There has thus been offered as a substitute for the present act a far broader and more effective set of provisions, which in no conceivable sense could breed trouble, but which to a far greater extent than the present act would both aid in making less likely a general war, and, while keeping strictly within the limits of neutrality, would reduce as far as possible the risk of this nation of being drawn into war if war comes.

In connection with our foreign affairs, I think all must agree that, unless a spirit of collaboration and cooperation characterizes the relations between the executive and legislative departments of the government, the peace and other vital interests of this country will inevitably be jeopardized.

Having spent the best years of my life as a member of the two Houses of Congress, I have the warmest feeling of friendliness toward the membership of, and the greatest respect for, the legislative department, and, in that spirit, I earnestly hope for the closest possible cooperation in matters affecting our country's best interests and its security in the present grave international situation.

At this time, when critical conditions obtain throughout the greater part of the world, I am sure that we are equally persuaded that, while the fullest measure of constructive criticism is helpful and desirable, and is of course most welcome, partisanship should play no part in the determination of the foreign policy of this country.

In the present situation of danger a peaceful nation like ours cannot complacently close its eyes and ears in formulating a peace and neutrality policy, as though abnormal and critical conditions did not exist.

The entire question of peace and neutrality at this serious juncture in its possible effects upon the safety and the interest of the United States during coming months is of the utmost importance. This question should, in my judgment, receive full and careful consideration and be acted upon by this government without unnecessary or undue delay.

CORDELL HULL.

APPENDIX 7

PRESIDENT ROOSEVELT'S RADIO ADDRESS OF SEPTEMBER 3, 1939[1]

Tonight my single duty is to speak to the whole of America.

Until 4:30 o'clock this morning I had hoped against hope that some miracle would prevent a devastating war in Europe and bring to an end the invasion of Poland by Germany.

For four long years a succession of actual wars and constant crises have shaken the entire world and have threatened in each case to bring on the gigantic conflict which is today unhappily a fact.

It is right that I should recall to your minds the consistent and at times successful efforts of your government in these crises to throw the full weight of the United States into the cause of peace. In spite of spreading wars I think that we have every right and every reason to maintain as a national policy the fundamental moralities, the teachings of religion and the continuation of efforts to restore peace—for some day, though the time may be distant, we can be of even greater help to a crippled humanity.

It is right, too, to point out that the unfortunate events of these recent years have been based on the use of force or the threat of force. And it seems to me clear, even at the outbreak of this great war, that the influence of America should be consistent in seeking for humanity a final peace which will eliminate, as far as it is possible to do so, the continued use of force between nations.

It is, of course, impossible to predict the future. I have my constant stream of information from American representatives and other sources throughout the world. You, the people of this country, are receiving news through your radios and your newspapers at every hour of the day.

[1] *New York Times,* September 4, 1939.

You are, I believe, the most enlightened and the best-informed people in all the world at this moment. You are subjected to no censorship of news, and I want to add that your government has no information which it has any thought of withholding from you.

At the same time, as I told my press conference on Friday, it is of the highest importance that the press and the radio use the utmost caution to discriminate between actual verified fact on the one hand and mere rumor on the other.

I can add to that by saying that I hope the people of this country will also discriminate most carefully between news and rumor. Do not believe of necessity everything you hear or read. Check up on it first.

You must master at the outset a simple but unalterable fact in modern foreign relations. When peace has been broken anywhere, peace of all countries everywhere is in danger.

It is easy for you and me to shrug our shoulders and say that conflicts taking place thousands of miles from the continental United States, and, indeed, the whole American Hemisphere, do not seriously affect the Americas, and that all the United States has to do is to ignore them and go about our own business.

Passionately though we may desire detachment, we are forced to realize that every word that comes through the air, every ship that sails the sea, every battle that is fought does affect the American future.

Let no man or woman thoughtlessly or falsely talk of America sending its armies to European fields. At this moment there is being prepared a proclamation of American neutrality. This would have been done even if there had been no neutrality statute on the books, for this proclamation is in accordance with international law and with American policy.

This will be followed by a proclamation required by the existing Neutrality Act. I trust that in the days to come our neutrality can be made a true neutrality.

It is of the utmost importance that the people of this country, with the best information in the world, think things through. The most dangerous enemies of American peace are those who, without well-rounded information on the whole broad subject of the past, the present and the future, undertake to speak with authority, to talk in terms of glittering generalities, to give to the nation assurances or prophecies which are of little present or future value.

I, myself, cannot and do not prophesy the course of events abroad—and the reason is that because I have of necessity such a complete picture of what is going on in every part of the world, I do not dare to do so. And the other reason is that I think it is honest for me to be honest with the people of the United States.

I cannot prophesy the immediate economic effect of this new war on our nation but I do say that no American has the moral right to profiteer at the expense of his fellow-citizens or of the men, women and children who are living and dying in the midst of war in Europe.

Some things we do know. Most of us in the United States believe in spiritual values. Most of us, regardless of what church we belong to, believe in the spirit of the New Testament—a great teaching which opposes itself to the use of force, of armed force, of marching armies and falling bombs. The overwhelming masses of our people seek peace —peace at home, and the kind of peace in other lands which will not jeopardize peace at home.

We have certain ideas and ideals of national safety and we must act to preserve that safety today and to preserve the safety of our children in future years.

That safety is, and will be, bound up with the safety of the Western Hemisphere and of the seas adjacent thereto. We seek to keep war from our firesides by keeping war from coming to the Americas.

For that we have historic precedent that goes back to the days of the administration of President George Washington.

It is serious enough and tragic enough to every American family in every State in the Union to live in a world that is torn by wars on other continents. Today they affect every American home. It is our national duty to use every effort to keep them out of the Americas.

And at this time let me make the simple plea that partisanship and selfishness be adjourned; and that national unity be the thought that underlies all others.

This nation will remain a neutral nation, but I cannot ask that every American remain neutral in thought as well. Even a neutral has a right to take account of facts. Even a neutral cannot be asked to close his mind or his conscience.

I have said not once but many times that I have seen war and that I hate war. I say that again and again.

I hope the United States will keep out of this war. I believe that it will. And I give you assurances that every effort of your government will be directed toward that end.

As long as it remains within my power to prevent it, there will be no blackout of peace in the United States.

APPENDIX 8

SECRETARY HULL'S DEPARTMENTAL ORDER OF SEPTEMBER 4, 1939, CONCERNING TRAVEL OF AMERICAN CITIZENS TO AND FROM EUROPE.[1]

By virtue of and pursuant to the authority vested in me by Section I of the Act of July 3, 1926, 44 Stat. 887 (U. S. C., Title 22, Section 211A), and by Executive Order No. 7856 of March 31, 1938, prescribing rules governing the granting and issuing of passports in the United States, I, the undersigned, Secretary of State of the United States, hereby prescribe the following regulations:

No passport heretofore issued shall be valid for use in traveling from the United States to any country in Europe unless it is submitted to the Department of State for validation.

Before the Department of State will validate any passport heretofore issued for use in any country in Europe, it will be necessary for the person to whom the passport was issued to submit documentary evidence concerning the imperativeness of his proposed travel. A person who desires travel in Europe for commercial purposes must support his application for the validation of his passport or for the issue of a passport with a letter from the head of the firm in the interests of which he intends to go to Europe. Such letter must state not only the names of the European countries which the applicant expects to visit and the objects of his visits thereto, but in addition, whether or not the applicant is a salaried employee of the firm concerned; and if so, how long he has been known to the firm and for what period of time he has been in its employ. If the applicant is going to Europe on a commission and not a salary basis, that fact

[1]Department of State Press Release.

also should be specifically stated. If the applicant for a passport is himself the head of the concern for which he is going to Europe, he must submit a letter from another officer of the concern or a letter from the head of some other reputable concern who has had business transactions with the applicant and has knowledge of the business in which the applicant is engaged and the object and necessity of his proposed trip to Europe.

An applicant who is going to Europe for any purpose other than commercial business must satisfy the Department of State that it is imperative that he go, and he must submit satisfactory documentary evidence substantiating his statement concerning the imperativeness of his proposed trip.

In view of the exigencies of the present situation and the consequent necessity of exercising the greatest care in the validation of passports or the issue of new passports, the Department of State will be obliged to hold applicants and firms responsible for any false or misleading statements made by them in connection with applications for passports, and any such false or misleading statements would be in violation of Section 220 of Title 22 of the United States Code, which reads as follows:

"Whoever shall willfully and knowingly make any false statement in an application for passport with intent to induce or secure the issuance of a passport under the authority of the United States, either for his own use or the use of another, contrary to the laws regulating the issuance of passports or the rules prescribed pursuant to such laws, or whoever shall willfully and knowingly use or attempt to use or furnish to another for use, any passport, the issue of which was secured in any way by reason of any false statement, shall be fined not more than $2,000 or imprisoned not more than five years or both."

Women and children will not be included in passports issued to their husbands or fathers unless the urgent and imperative necessity of accompanying them is conclusively established.

Passports will not, as a rule, be validated or issued for travel in opposing belligerent countries.

Should a person now having a valid passport proceed to any European country without first having submitted his passport to the Department of State for validation, the protection of the United States may be withheld from him while he is abroad.

Should a person to whom a passport has been issued use it in violation of the conditions or restrictions contained therein the protection of the United States may likewise be withheld from him while he is abroad and he will be liable for prosecution under the provisions of Section 221 of Title 22 of the U. S. Code, which reads in part as follows:

"* * * whoever shall willfully and knowingly use or attempt to use any passport in violation of the conditions or restrictions therein contained, or of the rules prescribed pursuant to the laws regulating the issuance of passports, which said rules shall be printed on the passport * * * shall be fined not more than $2,000 or imprisoned not more than five years, or both."

Hereafter when a passport is validated for or issued for use in Europe, its validity shall be restricted to the period necessary to accomplish the purpose of the intended visit to Europe but in no case beyond a period of six months.

Passports in possession of persons now residing abroad shall in due course be submitted to American consular officers for appropriate endorsement under special instructions to be sent to such officers at a later date.

CORDELL HULL

Department of State, September 4, 1939.

PRESIDENT ROOSEVELT'S PROCLAMATION OF NEUTRALITY, SEPTEMBER 5, 1939[1]

A Proclamation

Whereas a state of war unhappily exists between Germany and France; Poland; and the United Kingdom, India, Australia and New Zealand;

And whereas the United States is on terms of friendship and amity with the contending powers, and with the persons inhabiting their several dominions; and whereas there are nationals of the United States residing within the territories or dominions of each of the said belligerents, and carrying on commerce, trade, or other business or pursuits therein; and whereas there are nationals of each of the said belligerents residing within the territory or jurisdiction of the United States, and carrying on commerce, trade, or other business or pursuits therein; and whereas the laws and treaties of the United States, without interfering with the free expression of opinion and sympathy, nevertheless impose upon all persons who may be within their territory and jurisdiction the duty of an impartial neutrality during the existence of the contest;

And whereas it is the duty of a neutral government not to permit or suffer the making of its territory or territorial waters subservient to the purposes of war;

Now, therefore, I, Franklin D. Roosevelt, President of the United States of America, in order to preserve the neutrality of the United States and of its citizens and of persons within its territory and jurisdiction, and to enforce its laws and treaties, and in order that all persons, being warned of the general tenor of the laws and treaties of the United States in this behalf, and of the law of nations, may thus be prevented from any violation of the same, do hereby declare

[1]Department of State Press Release.

and proclaim that by certain provisions of the act approved on the 4th day of March, A. D., 1909, commonly known as the "Penal Code of the United States" and of the act approved on the 15th day of June, A. D. 1917, the following acts are forbidden to be done, under severe penalties, within the territory and jurisdiction of the United States, to wit:

1. Accepting and exercising a commission to serve one of the said belligerents by land or by sea against an opposing belligerent.

2. Enlisting or entering into the service of a belligerent as a soldier, or as a marine, or seaman on board of any ship of war, letter of marque, or privateer.

3. Hiring or retaining another person to enlist or enter himself in the service of a belligerent as a soldier, or as a marine, or seaman on board of any ship of war, letter of marque, or privateer.

4. Hiring another person to go beyond the limits or jurisdiction of the United States with intent to be enlisted as aforesaid.

5. Hiring another person to go beyond the limits or jurisdiction of the United States with intent to be entered into service as aforesaid.

6. Retaining another person to go beyond the limits or jurisdiction of the United States to be enlisted as aforesaid.

7. Retaining another person to go beyond the limits or jurisdiction of the United States with intent to be entered into service as aforesaid. (But the said act of the 4th day of March, A. D. 1909, as amended by the act of the 15th day of June A. D. 1917, is not to be construed to extend to a citizen or subject of a belligerent, who, being transiently within the jurisdiction of the United States, shall, on board of any ship of war, which, at the time of its arrival within the jurisdiction of the United States, was fitted and equipped as such ship of war, enlist or enter himself or hire or retain another subject or citizen of the same belligerent, who is

transiently within the jurisdiction of the United States, to enlist or enter himself to serve such belligerent on board such ship of war, if the United States shall then be at peace with such belligerent.)

8. Fitting out and arming, or attempting to fit out and arm, or procuring to be fitted out and armed, or knowingly being concerned in the furnishing, fitting out, or arming of any ship or vessel with intent that such ship or vessel shall be employed in the service of one of the said belligerents to cruise, or commit hostilities against the subjects, citizens, or property of an opposing belligerent.

9. Issuing or delivering a commission within the territory or jurisdiction of the United States for any ship or vessel to the intent that she may be employed as aforesaid.

10. Increasing or augmenting, or procuring to be increased or augmented, or knowingly being concerned in increasing or augmenting, the force of any ship of war, cruiser, or other armed vessel, which at the time of her arrival within the jurisdiction of the United States was a ship of war, cruiser, or armed vessel in the service of a belligerent, or belonging to a national thereof, by adding to the number of guns of such vessel, or by changing those on board of her for guns of a larger caliber, or by the addition thereto of any equipment solely applicable to war.

11. Knowingly beginning or setting on foot or providing or preparing a means for or furnishing the money for, or taking part in, any military or naval expedition or enterprise to be carried on from the territory or jurisdiction of the United States against the territory or dominion of a belligerent.

12. Despatching from the United States, or any place subject to the jurisdiction thereof, any vessel, domestic or foreign, which is about to carry to a warship, tender or supply ship of a belligerent any fuel, arms, ammunition, men, supplies, despatches or information shipped or received on board within the jurisdiction of the United States.

13. Despatching from the United States, or any place subject to the jurisdiction thereof, any armed vessel owned wholly or in part by American citizens, or any vessel, domestic or foreign (other than one which has entered the jurisdiction of the United States as a public vessel), which is manifestly built for warlike purposes or has been converted or adapted from a private vessel to one suitable for warlike use, and which is to be employed to cruise against or commit or attempt to commit hostilities upon the subjects, citizens, or property of a belligerent nation, or which will be sold or delivered to a belligerent nation, or to an agent, officer, or citizen thereof, within the jurisdiction of the United States, or, having left that jurisdiction, upon the high seas.

14. Despatching from the United States, or any place subject to the jurisdiction thereof, any vessel built, armed, or equipped as a ship of war, or converted from a private vessel into a ship of war (other than one which has entered the jurisdiction of the United States as a public vessel), with any intent or under any agreement or contract, written or oral, that such vessel shall be delivered to a belligerent nation, or to any agent, officer, or citizen of such nation, or where there is reasonable cause to believe that the said vessel shall or will be employed in the service of such belligerent nation after its departure from the jurisdiction of the United States.

15. Taking, or attempting or conspiring to take, or authorizing the taking of any vessel out of port or from the jurisdiction of the United States in violation of the said act of the 15th day of June, A. D. 1917, as set forth in the preceding paragraphs numbered 11 to 14 inclusive.

16. Leaving or attempting to leave the jurisdiction of the United States by a person belonging to the armed land or naval forces of a belligerent who shall have been interned within the jurisdiction of the United States in accordance with the law of nations, or leaving or attempting to leave the limits of internment in which freedom of movement has been allowed, without permission from the proper official of the

United States in charge, or wilfully overstaying a leave of absence granted by such official.

17. Aiding or enticing any interned person to escape or attempt to escape from the jurisdiction of the United States, or from the limits of internment prescribed.

And I do hereby further declare and proclaim that any frequenting and use of the waters within the territorial jurisdiction of the United States by the vessels of a belligerent, whether public ships or privateers for the purpose of preparing for hostile operations, or as posts of observation upon the ships of war or privateers or merchant vessels of an opposing belligerent must be regarded as unfriendly and offensive, and in violation of that neutrality which it is the determination of this government to observe; and to the end that the hazard and inconvenience of such apprehended practices may be avoided, I further proclaim and declare that from and after the fifth day of September instant, and so long as this proclamation shall be in effect, no ship of war or privateer of any belligerent shall be permitted to make use of any port, harbor, roadstead, or waters subject to the jurisdiction of the United States as a station or place of resort for any warlike purpose or for the purpose of obtaining warlike equipment; no privateer of a belligerent shall be permitted to depart from any port, harbor, roadstead or waters subject to the jurisdiction of the United States; and no ship of war of a belligerent shall be permitted to sail out or leave any port, harbor, roadstead, or waters subject to the jurisdiction of the United States from which a vessel of an opposing belligerent (whether the same shall be a ship of war or a merchant ship) shall have previously departed, until after the expiration of at least twenty-four hours from the departure of such last mentioned vessel beyond the jurisdiction of the United States.

If any ship of war of a belligerent shall, after the time this notification takes effect, be found in, or shall enter any port, harbor, roadstead, or waters subject to the jurisdiction of the United States, such vessel shall not be permitted to remain in such port, harbor, roadstead or waters more than twenty-four hours, except in case of stress of weather, or for delay in receiving supplies or repairs, or when detained by the United States; in any of which cases the authorities of the port, or of the nearest port (as the case may be), shall require her to put to sea as soon as the cause of the delay is at an end, unless within the preceding twenty-four hours a vessel, whether ship of war or merchant ship of an opposing belligerent, shall have departed therefrom, in which case the time limit for the departure of such ship of war shall be extended so far as may be necessary to secure an interval of not less than twenty-four hours between such departure and that of any ship of war or merchant ship of an opposing belligerent which may have previously quit the same port, harbor, roadstead, or waters.

Vessels used exclusively for scientific, religious, or philanthropic purposes are exempted from the foregoing provisions as to the length of time ships of war may remain in the ports, harbors, roadsteads, or waters subject to the jurisdiction of the United States.

The maximum number of ships of war belonging to a belligerent and its allies which may be in one of the ports, harbors or roadsteads subject to the jurisdiction of the United States simultaneously shall be three.

When ships of war of opposing belligerents are present simultaneously in the same port, harbor, roadstead, or waters, subject to the jurisdiction of the United States, the one entering first shall depart first, unless she is in such condition as to warrant extending her stay. In any case the ship which arrived later has the right to notify the other through the competent local authority that within twenty-four hours she will leave such port, harbor, roadstead, or waters, the one first entering, however, having the right to depart within that time. If the one first entering leaves, the notifying ship must observe the prescribed interval of twenty-four hours. If a delay beyond twenty-four hours from the time of arrival is granted, the termination of the cause of delay will be considered the time of arrival in deciding the right of priority in departing.

Vessels of a belligerent shall not be permitted to depart successively from any port, harbor, roadstead, or waters subject to the jurisdiction of the United States at such intervals as will delay the departure of a ship of war of an opposing belligerent from such ports, harbors, roadsteads, or waters for more than twenty-four hours beyond her desired time of sailing. If, however, the departure of several ships of war and merchant ships of opposing belligerents from the same port, harbor, roadstead, or waters is involved, the order of their departure therefrom shall be so arranged as to acord the opportunity of leaving alternately to the vessels of the opposing belligerents, and to cause the least detention consistent with the objects of this proclamation.

All belligerent vessels shall refrain from use of their radio and signal apparatus while in the harbors, ports, roadsteads, or waters subject to the jurisdiction of the United States, except for calls of distress and communications connected with safe navigation or arrangements for the arrival of the vessel within, or departure from, such harbors, ports, roadsteads, or waters, or passage through such waters; provided that such communications will not be of direct material aid to the belligerent in the conduct of military operations against an opposing belligerent. The radio of belligerent merchant vessels may be sealed by the authorities of the United States, and such seals shall not be broken within the jurisdiction of the United States except by proper authority of the United States.

No ship of war of a belligerent shall be permitted, while in any port, harbor, roadstead, or waters subject to the jurisdiction of the United States, to take in any supplies except provisions and such other things as may be requisite for the subsistence of her crew in amounts necessary to bring such supplies to her peace standard, and except such fuel, lubricants, and feed water only as may be sufficient, with that already on board, to carry such vessel, if without any sail power, to the nearest port of her own country; or in case a vessel is rigged to go under sail, and may also be propelled by machinery, then half the quantity of fuels, lubricants, and feed water which she would be entitled to have on board, if dependent upon propelling machinery alone, and no fuel, lubricants, or feed water shall be again supplied to any such ship of war in the same or any other port, harbor, roadstead, or waters subject to the jurisdiction of the United States until after the expiration of three months from the time when such fuel, lubricants and feed water may have been last supplied to her within waters subject to the jurisdiction of the United States. The amounts of fuel, lubricants, and feed water allowable under the above provisions shall be based on the economical speed of the vessel, plus an allowance of thirty per centum for eventualities.

No ship of war of a belligerent shall be permitted, while in any port, harbor, roadstead, or waters subject to the jurisdiction of the United States, to make repairs beyond those that are essential to render the vessel seaworthy and which in no degree constitute an increase in her military strength. Repairs shall be made without delay. Damages which are found to have been produced by the enemy's fire shall in no case be repaired.

No ship of war of a belligerent shall effect repairs or receive fuel, lubricants, feed water, or provisions within the jurisdiction of the United States without written authorization of the proper authorities of the United States. Before such authorization will be issued, the commander of the vessel shall furnish to such authorities a written declaration, duly signed by such commander, stating the date, port, and amounts of supplies last received in the jurisdiction of the United States, the amounts of fuel, lubricants, feed water, and provisions on board, the port to which the vessel is proceeding, the economical speed of the vessel, the rate of consumption of fuel, lubricants, and feed water at such speed, and the amount of each class of supplies desired. If repairs are desired, a similar declaration shall be furnished stating the cause of the damage and the nature of the repairs. In either case, a certificate shall be included to the effect that the desired services are in accord with the rules of the United States in that behalf.

No agency of the United States Government shall, directly or indirectly, provide supplies nor effect repairs to a belligerent ship of war.

No vessel of a belligerent shall exercise the right of search within the waters under the jurisdiction of the United States, nor shall prizes be taken by belligerent vessels within such waters. Subject to any applicable treaty provisions in force, prizes captured by belligerent vessels shall not enter any port, harbor, roadstead, or waters under the jurisdiction of the United States except in case of unseaworthiness, stress of weather, or want of fuel or provisions; when the cause has disappeared, the prize must leave immediately, and if a prize captured by a belligerent vessel enters any port, harbor, roadstead, or waters subject to the jurisdiction of the United States for any other reason than on account of unseaworthiness, stress of weather, or want of fuel or provisions, or fails to leave as soon as the circumstances which justified the entrance are at an end, the prize with its officers and crew will be released and the prize crew will be interned. A belligerent prize court can not be set up on territory subject to the jurisdiction of the United States or on a vessel in the ports, harbors, roadsteads, or waters subject to the jurisdiction of the United States.

The provisions of this proclamation pertaining to ships of war shall apply equally to any vessel operating under public control for hostile or military purposes.

And I do further declare and proclaim that the statutes and the treaties of the United States and the law of nations alike require that no person, within the territory and jurisdiction of the United States, shall take part, directly or indirectly, in the said war, but shall remain at peace with all of the said belligerents, and shall maintain a strict and impartial neutrality.

And I do further declare and proclaim that the provisions of this proclamation shall apply to the Canal Zone except in so far as such provisions may be specifically modified by a proclamation or proclamations issued for the Canal Zone.

And I do hereby enjoin all nationals of the United States, and all persons residing or being within the territory or jurisdiction of the United States, to observe the laws thereof, and to commit no act contrary to the provisions of the said statutes or treaties or in violation of the law of nations in that behalf.

And I do hereby give notice that all nationals of the United States and others who may claim the protection of this government, who may misconduct themselves in the premises, will do so at their peril, and that they can in no wise obtain any protection from the government of the United States against the consequences of their misconduct.

This proclamation shall continue in full force and effect unless and until modified, revoked or otherwise terminated, pursuant to law.

In witness whereof, I have hereunto set my hand and caused the seal of the United States to be affixed.

Done at the city of Washington this fifth day of September in the year of our Lord nineteen hundred and thirty-nine, and of the Independence of the United States of America the one hundred and sixty-fourth.

FRANKLIN D. ROOSEVELT.

By the President:

CORDELL HULL
    Secretary of State.

APPENDIX 10

PRESIDENT ROOSEVELT'S PROCLAMATION OF SEPTEMBER 5, 1939, CONCERNING THE EXPORT OF ARMS, AMMUNITION, AND IMPLEMENTS OF WAR TO FRANCE, GERMANY, POLAND, THE UNITED KINGDOM, INDIA, AUSTRALIA AND NEW ZEALAND[1]

Whereas section 1 of the joint resolution of Congress approved May 1, 1937, provides in part as follows:

"Whenever the President shall find that there exists a state of war between, or among, two or more foreign states, the President shall proclaim such fact, and it shall thereafter be unlawful to export, or attempt to export, or cause to be exported, arms, ammunition, or implements of war from any place in the United States to any belligerent state named in such proclamation, or to any neutral state for transshipment to, or for the use of, any such belligerent state."

And whereas it is further provided by section 1 of the said joint resolution that

"The President shall, from time to time by proclamation, definitely enumerate the arms, ammunition and implements of war, the export of which is prohibited by this section. The arms, ammunition and implements of war so enumerated shall include those enumerated in the President's proclamation numbered 2163, of April 10, 1936, but shall not include raw materials or any other articles or materials not of the same general character as those enumerated in the said proclamation, and in the Convention for the Supervision of the International Trade in Arms and Ammunition and in Implements of War, signed at Geneva June 17, 1925."

And whereas it is further provided by section 1 of the said joint resolution that

[1]Department of State Press Release. By additional proclamations this Proclamation was subsequently extended to include Union of South Africa and Canada.

"Whoever, in violation of any of the provisions of this Act, shall export, or attempt to export, or cause to be exported, arms, ammunition, or implements of war from the United States shall be fined not more than $10,000 or imprisoned not more than five years, or both, and the property, vessel, or vehicle containing the same shall be subject to the provisions of sections 1 to 8, inclusive, title 6, chapter 30, of the Act approved June 15, 1917 (40 Stat. 223-225; U. S. C., 1934 ed., title 22, secs. 238-245)."

And whereas it is further provided by section 1 of the said joint resolution that

"In the case of the forfeiture of any arms, ammunition, or implements of war by reason of a violation of this Act, no public or private sale shall be required; but such arms, ammunition, or implements of war shall be delivered to the Secretary of War for such use or disposal thereof as shall be approved by the President of the United States."

And whereas it is further provided by section 11 of the said joint resolution that

"The President may, from time to time, promulgate such rules and regulations, not inconsistent with law, as may be necessary and proper to carry out any of the provisions of this act; and he may exercise any power or authority conferred on him by this act through such officer or officers, or agency or agencies, as he shall direct."

Now, therefore, I, Franklin D. Roosevelt, President of the United States of America, acting under and by virtue of the authority conferred on me by the said joint resolution, do hereby proclaim that a state of war unhappily exists between Germany and France; Poland; and the United Kingdom, India, Australia and New Zealand, and I do hereby admonish all citizens of the United States, or any of its possessions, and all persons residing or being within the territory or jurisdiction of the United States, or its possessions, to abstain from every violation of the provisions of the joint resolution above set forth, hereby made effective and applicable to the export of arms, ammunition, or implements of war from any place in the United States or any of its possessions to France; Germany; Poland; or the United Kingdom, India, Australia and New Zealand, or to any other State for transshipment to, or for the use of, France; Germany; Poland; or the United Kingdom, India, Australia and New Zealand.

And I do hereby declare and proclaim that the articles enumerated below shall be considered arms, ammunition and enumerated of war for the purposes of section 1 of the said joint resolution of Congress:

CATEGORY 1

(1) Rifles and carbines using ammunition in excess of caliber .22, and barrels for those weapons;

(2) Machine guns, automatic or autoloading rifles, and machine pistols using ammunition in excess of caliber .22, and barrels for those weapons;

(3) Guns, howitzers, and mortars of all calibers, their mountings and barrels;

(4) Ammunition in excess of caliber .22 for the arms enumerated under (1) and (2) above, and cartridge cases or bullets for such ammunition; filled and unfilled projectiles for the arms enumerated under (3) above;

(5) Grenades, bombs, torpedoes, mines and depth charges, filled or unfilled, and apparatus for their use or discharge;

(6) Tanks, military armored vehicles, and armored trains.

CATEGORY II

Vessels of war of all kinds, including aircraft carriers and submarines, and armor plate for such vessels.

CATEGORY III

(1) Aircraft, unassembled, assembled, or dismantled, both heavier and lighter than air, which are designed, adapted, and intended for aerial combat by the use of machine guns or of artillery or for the carrying and dropping of bombs, or which are equipped with, or which by reason of design or construction are prepared for, any of the appliances referred to in paragraph (2) below:

(2) Aerial gun mounts and frames, bomb racks, torpedo carriers, and bomb or torpedo release mechanisms.

CATEGORY IV

(1) Revolvers and automatic pistols using ammunition in excess of caliber .22.

(2) Ammunition in excess of caliber .22 for the arms enumerated under (1) above, and cartridge cases or bullets for such ammunition.

CATEGORY V

(1) Aircraft, unassembled, assembled or dismantled, both heavier and lighter than air, other than those included in Category III.

(2) Propellers or air screws, fuselages, hulls, wings, tail units, and under-carriage units.

(3) Aircraft engines, unassembled, assembled, or dismantled.

CATEGORY VI

(1) Livens projectors and flame throwers;
(2) a. Mustard gas (dichlorethyl sulphide);
    b. Lewisite (chlorvinyldichlorarsine and dichlordivinylchlorarsine);
    c. Methyldichlorarsine;

d. Diphenylchlorarsine;
e. Diphenylcyanarsine;
f. Diphenylaminechlorarsine;
g. Phenyldichlorarsine;
h. Ethyldichlorarsine;
i. Phenyldibromarsine;
j. Ethyldibromarsine;
k. Phosgene;
l. Monochlormethylchlorformate;
m. Trichlormethylchlorformate (diphosgene);
n. Dichlordimethyl ether;
o. Dibromdimethyl ether;
p. Cyanogen chloride;
q. Ethylbromacetate;
r. Ethyliodoacetate;
s. Brombenzylcyanide;
t. Bromacetone;
u. Brommethylethyl ketone.

Category VII

(1) Propellant powders;
(2) High explosives as follows:
   a. Nitrocellulose having a nitrogen content of more than 12 per cent;
   b. Trinitrotoluene;
   c. Trinitroxylene;
   d. Tetryl (trinitrophenol methyl nitramine or tetranitro methylaniline);
   e. Picric acid;
   f. Ammonium picrate;
   g. Trinitroanisol;

h. Trinitronaphthalene;

i. Teteranitronaphthalene;

j. Hexanitrodiphenylamine;

k. Pentaerythritetetranitrate (penthrite or pentrite);

l. Trimethylenetrinitramine (hexogen or T4);

m. Potassium nitrate powders (black saltpeter powder);

n. Sodium nitrate powders (black soda powder);

o. Amatol (mixture of ammonium nitrate and trinitrotoluene);

p. Ammonal (mixture of ammonium nitrate, trinitrotoluene and powdered aluminum, with or without other ingredients);

q. Schneiderite (mixture of ammonium nitrate and dinitronaphthalene, with or without other ingredients).

And I do hereby enjoin upon all officers of the United States, charged with the execution of the law thereof, the utmost diligence in preventing violations of the said joint resolution, and this my proclamation issued thereunder, and in bringing to trial and punishment any offenders against the same.

And I do hereby delegate to the Secretary of State the power to exercise any power or authority conferred on me by the said joint resolution, as made effective by this my proclamation issued thereunder, and the power to promulgate such rules and regulations not inconsistent with law as may be necessary and proper to carry out any of its provisions.

In witness whereof, I have hereunto set my hand and caused the seal of the United States of America to be affixed.

Done at the city of Washington this fifth day of September, in the year of Our Lord nineteen hundred and thirty-nine, and of the Independence of the United States of America the one hundred and sixty-fourth.

(Seal).   FRANKLIN D. ROOSEVELT.

APPENDIX 11

REGULATIONS RESTRICTING TRAVEL OF AMERICAN CITIZENS ON VESSELS OF BELLIGERENT NATIONS, SEPTEMBER 5, 1939[1].

Section 9 of the joint resolution of Congress approved May 1, 1937, amending the joint resolution approved August 31, 1935, provides as follows:

"Whenever the President shall have issued a proclamation under the authority of section 1 of this Act it shall thereafter be unlawful for any citizen of the United States to travel on any vessel of the state or states named in such proclamation, except in accordance with such rules and regulations as the President shall prescribe;

"Provided, however, that the provisions of this section shall not apply to a citizen of the United States traveling on a vessel whose voyage was begun in advance of the date of the President's proclamation, and who had no opportunity to discontinue his voyage after that date: And provided further, that they shall not apply under ninety days after the date of the President's proclamation to a citizen of the United States returning from a foreign state to the United States.

"Whenever, in the President's judgment, the conditions which have caused him to issue his proclamation have ceased to exist, he shall revoke his proclamation and the provisions of this section shall thereupon cease to apply with respect to the state or states named in such proclamation, except with respect to offenses committed prior to such revocation."

Section 12 of the said joint resolution provides as follows:

"In every case of the violation of any of the provisions of this Act or of any rule or regulation issued pursuant thereto where a specific penalty is not herein provided, such violator or violators, upon conviction, shall be fined not more than $10,000, or imprisoned not more than five years, or both."

[1]Department of State Press Release.

Section 11 of the said joint resolution provides as follows:

"The President may, from time to time, promulgate such rules and regulations, not inconsistent with law, as may be necessary and proper to carry out any of the provisions of this Act; and he may exercise any power or authority conferred on him by this Act through such officer or officers, or agency or agencies, as he shall direct."

The President's proclamation of Sept. 5, 1939, issued pursuant to the provisions of section 1 of the above-mentioned joint resolution, provides in part as follows:

"And I do hereby delegate to the Secretary of State the power to exercise any power or authority conferred on me by the said joint resolution, as made effective by this my proclamation issued thereunder, and the power to promulgate such rules and regulations not inconsistent with law as may be necessary and proper to carry out any of its provisions."

In pursuance of those provisions of the law and of the President's proclamation of September 5, 1939, which are quoted above, the Secretary of State announces the following regulations:

American diplomatic and consular officers and their families, members of their staffs and their familities, and American military and naval officers and personnel and their families may travel pursuant to orders on vessels of France; Germany; Poland; or the United Kingdom, India, Australia and New Zealand if the public service requires.

Other American citizens may travel on vessels of France; Germany; Poland; or the United Kingdom, India, Australia and New Zealand; provided, however, that travel on or over the north Atlantic Ocean, east of 30 degrees west and north of 30 degrees north or on or over other waters adjacent to Europe or over the continent of Europe or adjacent islands shall not be permitted except when specifically authorized by the Secretary of State in each case.

CORDELL HULL
Secretary of State.

APPENDIX 12

REGULATIONS GOVERNING THE COLLECTION OF CONTRIBUTIONS FOR USE IN THE BELLIGERENT COUNTRIES, SEPTEMBER 5, 1939[1]

Section 3 of the joint resolution of Congress approved May 1, 1937, (Public Resolution—No. 27—75th Congress—First Session) amending the joint resolution approved August 31, 1935, as amended, provides in part as follows:

(a) Whenever the President shall issued a proclamation under the authority of section 1 of this Act, it shall thereafter be unlawful for any person within the United States to purchase, sell, or exchange bonds, securities, or other obligations of the government of any belligerent state or of any state wherein civil strife exists, named in such proclamation, or of any political subdivision of any such state, or of any person acting for or on behalf of the government of any such state, or of any faction or asserted government within any such state wherein civil strife exists, or of any person acting for or on behalf of any faction or asserted government within any such state wherein civil strife exists, issued after the date of such proclamation, or to make any loan or extend any credit to any such government, political subdivision, faction, asserted government or person, *or to solicit or receive any contribution for any such government, political subdivision, faction, asserted government or person: Provided, That * * * Nothing in this subsection shall be construed to prohibit the solicitation or collection of funds to be used for medical aid and assistance, or for food and clothing to relieve human suffering, when such solicitation or collection of funds is made on behalf of and for use by any person or organization which is not acting for or on behalf of any such government, political subdivision, faction, or asserted government, but all such solicitations and collections of funds shall be subject to the approval of the President and shall be made under rules and regulations as he shall prescribe.* (Italics supplied.)

*　　*　　*　　*　　*　　*

(c) Whoever shall violate the provisions of this section or of any regulations issued hereunder shall, upon conviction thereof, be fined not more than $50,000 or imprisoned for not more than five years, or both. Should the violation be by a corporation, organiza-

[1]Department of State Press Release.

tion, or association, each officer or agent thereof participating in the violation may be liable to the penalty herein prescribed.

On September 5, 1939, the President issued a proclamation in respect to France; Germany; Poland; and the United Kingdom, India, Australia and New Zealand, under the authority of section 1 of the said joint resolution, thereby making effective in respect to those countries the provisions of section 3 of the said joint resolution quoted above.

Section 11 of the said joint resolution provides as follows:

SEC. 11. The President may, from time to time, promulgate such rules and regulations, not inconsistent with law, as may be necessary and proper to carry out any of the provisions of this Act; and he may exercise any power or authority conferred on him by this Act through such officer or officers, or agency or agencies, as he shall direct.

The President's proclamation of September 5, 1939, referred to above, issued pursuant to the provisions of section 1 of the above-mentioned joint resolution provides in part as follows:

And I do hereby delegate to the Secretary of State the power to exercise any power or authority conferred on me by the said joint resolution, as made effective by this my proclamation issued thereunder, and the power to promulgate such rules and regulations not inconsistent with law as may be necessary and proper to carry out any of its provisions.

In pursuant of those provisions of the law and of the President's proclamation of September 5, 1939, which are referred to above, the Secretary of State promulgates the following regulations:

(1) The term "person" as used herein and in the Act of May 1, 1937, includes a partnership, company, association, organization or corporation as well as a natural person.

(2) Any person within the United States, its territories, insular possessions (including the Philippine Islands), the Canal Zone, and the District of Columbia who desires to engage in the solicitation or collection of contributions to be used for medical aid and assistance in France; Germany; Poland; or the United Kingdom, India, Australia, and New

Zealand, or for food and clothing to relieve human suffering in any of those countries, and who is not acting for or on behalf of the governments of France; Germany; Poland; or the United Kingdom, India, Australia and New Zealand, or any political subdivision of any of such countries, shall register with the Secretary of State. To this end, such person shall make application to the Secretary of State upon the form provided therefor.

(3) Organizations or associations having chapters shall list them in their application for registration and shall set forth therein the addresses of such chapters. In case chapters are formed after the registration of the parent organization, the parent should immediately inform the Secretary of State in order that its registration may be amended to name the new chapter or chapters.

(4) No person shall solicit or collect contributions without having in his possession a notice from the Secretary of State of acceptance of registration which has not been revoked; Provided, however, that nothing in this regulation shall be construed as requiring a duly authorized agent of a registrant to have in his possession a notice of acceptance of registration. Chapters named in the parent organization's registration may, of course, operate under this registration. Notices of acceptance of registration shall not be exhibited, used, or referred to, in any manner which might be construed as implying official endorsement of the persons engaged in the solicitation or collection of contributions.

(5) All persons registered with the Secretary of State must maintain for his inspection or that of his duly authorized agent, complete records of all transactions in which the registrant engages.

(6) Persons receiving notification of acceptance of registration shall submit to the Secretary of State not later than the tenth day of every month following the receipt of such notification sworn statements, in duplicate, on the form

provided therefor setting forth fully the information called for therein.

(7) The Secretary of State reserves the right to reject applications or to revoke registrations for failure on the part of the registrant to comply with the provisions or purposes of the law or of these regulations.

(8) A registrant may act as an agent for the transmittal abroad of funds received by another registrant, but such funds shall not be accountable as contributions received by the transmitting registrant.

(9) Any changes in the facts set forth in the registrant's application for registration, such as change of address, of officers, or of means of distribution abroad, should be reported promptly to the Secretary of State in the form of a supplemental application, in duplicate, properly sworn to.

(10) In view of the purposes and special status of "The American Red Cross" as set forth in the Act of Congress approved January 5, 1905, entitled "An Act to incorporate the American National Red Cross" (33 Stat. 599), and particularly in view of the fact that it is required by law to submit to the Secretary of War for audit "a full, complete, and itemized report of receipts and expenditures of whatever kind", so that the submission to the Secretary of State of reports of funds received and expended would constitute an unnecessary duplication, "The American National Red Cross" is not required to conform to the provisions of these regulations.

CORDELL HULL
Secretary of State

APPENDIX 13

REGULATION CONCERNING CREDITS TO
BELLIGERENTS, SEPTEMBER 6, 1939[1]

Section 3 of the joint resolution of Congress approved May 1, 1937, reads in part as follows:

SEC. 3. (a) Whenever the President shall have issued a proclamation under the authority of section 1 of this Act, it shall thereafter be unlawful for any person within the United States to purchase, sell, or exchange bonds, securities, or other obligations of the government of any belligerent state or of any state wherein civil strife exists, named in such proclamation, or of any political subdivision of any such state, or of any person acting for or on behalf of the government of any such state, or of any faction or asserted government within any such state wherein civil strife exists, or of any person acting for or on behalf of any faction or asserted government within any such state wherein civil strife exists, issued after the date of such proclamation, or to make any loan or extend any credit to any such government, political subdivision, faction, asserted government, or person, or to solicit or receive any contribution for any such government, political subdivision, faction, asserted government, or person: *Provided,* That if the President shall find that such action will serve to protect the commercial or other interests of the United States or its citizens, he may, in his discretion, and to such extent and under such regulations as he may prescribe, except from the operation of this section ordinary commercial credits and short-time obligations in aid of legal transactions and of a character customarily used in normal peacetime commercial transactions. Nothing in this subsection shall be construed to prohibit the solicitation or collection of funds to be used for medical aid and assistance, or for food and clothing to relieve human suffering, when such solicitation or collection of funds is made on behalf of and for use by any person or organization which is not acting for or on behalf of any such government, political subdivision, faction, or asserted government, but all such solicitations and collections of funds shall be subject to the approval of the President and shall be made under such rules and regulations as he shall prescribe.

[1] Department of State Press Release.

230

(b) The provisions of this section shall not apply to a renewal or adjustment of such indebtedness as may exist on the date of the President's proclamation.

(c) Whoever shall violate the provisions of this section or of any regulations issued hereunder shall, upon conviction thereof, be fined not more than $50,000 or imprisoned for not more than five years, or both. Should the violation be by a corporation, organization, or association, each officer or agent thereof participating in the violation may be liable to the penalty herein prescribed.

I hereby find that it will serve to protect the commercial and other interests of the United States and its citizens to except from the operation of Section 3 of the joint resolution of Congress approved May 1, 1937, as made applicable to Germany and France, Poland, and the United Kingdom, India, Australia and New Zealand by the Proclamation of the President of September 5, 1939 issued under the authority of Section 1 of such joint resolution, ordinary commercial credits and short-time obligations in aid of legal transactions and of a character customarily used in normal peace-time commercial transactions; and they are therefore hereby excepted.

I hereby authorize the Secretary of the Treasury to administer the provisions of this regulation and to promulgate such rules and regulations not inconsistent with law as may be necessary and proper to carry out such provisions.

This regulation shall continue in full force and effect unless and until modified, revoked, or otherwise terminated, pursuant to law.

FRANKLIN D. ROOSEVELT

THE WHITE HOUSE
        September 6, 1939.

APPENDIX 14

SECRETARY HULL'S STATEMENT OF
SEPTEMBER 14, 1939[1]

The Government of the United States has not abandoned any of its rights as a neutral under international law.

It has, however, for the time being prescribed, by domestic legislation, certain restrictions for its nationals which have the effect of requiring them to refrain from the exercise of privileges which but for such legislation they would have the right to exercise under international law, such as the right to travel on belligerent vessels, to make loans and extend credits to belligerent governments, et cetera.

These restrictive measures do not and can not constitute a modification of the principles of international law, but rather they require nationals of the United States to forego, until the Congress shall decide otherwise, the exercise of certain rights under those principles.

Furthermore, this Government gives the widest possible notice to American shipping regarding danger areas as the information is acquired by it. This Government also warns American nationals and American shipping against actual danger in any other respect as situations involving such danger are brought to its attention, whether those situations result from lawful or unlawful activities of the belligerents. It endeavors to exercise all due diligence in the protection of American lives and property and of course must expect American nationals likewise to exercise due diligence in keeping clear of danger—actual or potential.

In the letters which I addressed to Senator Pittman and Representative Bloom on May 27, 1939 I stated the situation as follows:

"The rights of our nationals under international law may properly be restricted by our own legislation along certain

[1]Department of State Press Release.

lines for the purpose of avoiding incidents which might involve us in a conflict. In indicating certain restrictions upon the exercise of our rights as a neutral I do not wish to be considered as advocating the abandonment of these, or indeed of any, neutral rights; but there is reasonable ground for restricting at this time the exercise of these rights."

The principles of international law as regards neutrals and belligerents have been evolved through the centuries. While belligerents have frequently departed from these principles on one pretext or another, and have endeavored to justify their action on various grounds, the principles still subsist.

This Government, adhering as it does to these principles, reserves all rights of the United States and its nationals under international law and will adopt such measures as may seem most practical and prudent when those rights are violated by any of the belligerents.

APPENDIX 15

A NOTE ON PREVIOUS AMERICAN EMBARGOES
OF ARMS SHIPMENTS

Arms embargoes have been employed by the United States Government mainly as a means of promoting political stability in neighboring republics. President Theodore Roosevelt established a precedent for such action in 1905. He based his authority on a Joint Resolution of April 22, 1898, enacted on the eve of the Spanish-American War and authorizing the President "in his discretion, and with such limitations and exceptions as to himself may seem expedient, to prohibit the export of coal and other material used in war from any seaport of the United States until otherwise ordered by Congress."[1]

The original object of this legislation was to prevent military supplies from being shipped from the United States to places where they might become available to Spanish forces in the Caribbean; but President Roosevelt found the measure useful for another purpose. In response to the appeal of President Morales of the Dominican Republic, he established a financial receivership for that country in order to relieve its government of the pressure of foreign creditors whose procedure incidentally threatened to impinge upon the Monroe Doctrine. To prevent these financial arrangements from being upset by revolution in the Dominican Republic, President Roosevelt utilized his powers under the war legislation of 1898 and forbade the "export of arms, ammunition and munitions of war of every kind" to that country.

The authority which Mr. Roosevelt thus exercised was made more specific by new legislation in 1912, when Congress also repealed the embargo measure of 1898. A Joint

[1]30 U. S. Statutes, 339. See also *Congressional Record*, Seventy-third Congress, First Session, 1743.

234

Resolution of March 14 empowered the President to prohibit the exportation of arms or munitions of war to any American country in which there were "conditions of domestic violence," and where such conditions might be aggravated "by the use of arms or munitions of war procured from the United States." By a second Joint Resolution of January 31, 1922, the President's power was extended to countries in which the United States exercised extraterritorial jurisdiction—specifically, to China.

Immediately after his approval of the Joint Resolution of 1912, President Taft imposed an embargo on shipments of arms to Mexico because of the revolutionary disturbances in that country. In 1914, President Wilson lifted the embargo in order that shipments might reach the Carranza government, which he was disposed to favor in preference to the government of Huerta. The Carranza government in northern Mexico was cut off by its opponents from access to the sea and could obtain military supplies only from the United States, while the Huerta government could import arms and munitions from Europe. The embargo on shipments to Mexico was re-employed in 1915, 1919 and 1924. On March 4, 1922, President Harding issued a proclamation extending the embargo to China. Similar proclamations, which were still in effect in 1935, were issued with respect to Honduras on March 22, 1924; with respect to Nicaragua on September 15, 1926; and with respect to Cuba on June 29, 1934. Under these provisions the exportation of arms to China, Cuba, Honduras and Nicaragua are permitted only when the Department of State has been informed by the diplomatic representatives of these countries that such shipments are desired by the governments of the respective countries.

On May 28, 1934, Congress passed a Joint Resolution authorizing the President to prohibit the sale of arms and munitions of war "to those countries now engaged in armed conflict in the Chaco," namely Bolivia and Paraguay. On the same day, President Franklin D. Roosevelt issued a proclamation making effective an embargo on arms shipments to these countries. This embargo remained in effect until November 29, 1935, when it was lifted because the war in the Chaco was officially ended.

The United States Government has usually employed its arms embargo in the case of revolutions in Latin American countries with a view to aiding one of the parties or ending a war rather than with a view to maintaining strict impartiality between the disputants. Following the precedent established by President Wilson in 1914, President Coolidge in 1926 allowed the adherents of the Diaz government in Nicaragua to obtain munitions in the United States while withholding them from the opponents of the Diaz régime. On several occasions, notably in 1924 and 1929, the United States has sold arms to the existing government in Mexico when it was threatened with revolution.

Early in 1933 an effort was made in Congress to give the President authority to declare an embargo on arms shipments to any country where such shipments might promote "the employment of force in the course of a dispute or conflict between nations." A Joint Resolution to this effect passed the Senate on January 19, 1933, but the House failed to act before Congress adjourned. When the new Congress convened in special session the House passed the resolution on April 17 by a vote of 253 to 109. In the Senate, however, the resolution was amended so as to make the embargo apply impartially to all the disputants. The Administration made no effort to obtain the passage of the measure in this form.

WILLIAM O. SCROGGS.

APPENDIX 16

CHANGES IN AMERICAN EXPORT TRADE, 1913-1937[1]

	Wheat and Flour[2] (1,000 bus.)	Cotton, excl. Linters[3] (1,000 bales)	Crude Foodstuffs (in $1,000)	Finished Mfrs. (in $1,000)
1913	154,768	8,544	181,907	776,297
1914	231,324	6,084	137,495	724,908
1928	206,258	7,542	294,677	2,260,002
1929	163,688	8,044	269,590	2,531,823
1930	153,247	6,690	178,533	1,898,089
1931	131,477	6,760	127,072	1,119,657
1932	135,799	8,708	89,419	624,228
1933	41,211	8,419	48,366	616,639
1934	37,002	7,534	59,032	878,839
1935	21,532	4,799	58,751	994,308
1936	15,929	5,973	58,144	1,154,099
1937	21,584	5,440	104,506	1,616,548

[1]Source, "Statistical Abstract of the United States."
[2]Flour converted to grain at rate of 4.7 bushels to barrel.
[3]Linters included prior to 1921.

APPENDIX 17—KEY WAR MATERIALS

PERCENTAGES OF WORLD PRODUCTION BY COUNTRIES, 1937

	United States	Great Britain	Canada	South Africa	Australia	British India	Malay States	Other British	France	Germany	Soviet Russia	Italy	Belgium	Belgian Congo	Norway	Sweden	Switzerland	Greece	Hungary	Jugoslavia	Rumania	Spain[2]	D. E. Indies	Siam	China[2]	Japan	Argentina	Bolivia	Brazil	Chile	Cuba	Mexico	Peru	Venezuela	All Other
Minerals																																			
Aluminum	27	4	9						7	26		5			5		3									2									3
Bauxite	11			18				9	18	2	7	10						4	14	9															11
Chromite[1]				18		5		18			22							5		5	1			5		4					7				16
Copper	36		9	1	2	1	1	3		3	14			7						1						4				17	7	2	1		18
Gold	11		11	34	4	2	1	10			16			1												4		1		1		2	3		18
Iron Ore[1]	29	7	1	1	2	5			19	4	15		1			7				1						1									13
Pig Iron	38	9	11	1	2	16		2	8	16	3	1	4			1						2				2									3
Lead	25	2		15	15	1		8	8	5	60	2	4							4							1	1				13	1		6
Manganese[1]				5	16																3				6	1			3						5
Nickel			90																																9
Nitrates (nat.)	10																													100					
Potash	62					3			19	57	10								2	2	1					1	1					2	1		4
Petroleum							38	5			10									2	19		3		6	1	1			1			1	10	8
Tin[1]		1		2		22	8	1												2			19	8	1			12							1
Tungsten[1]	9			2				43						4						1		2	8		39	6	3	7	3						9
Vanadium	26																																31		
Other Key Materials																																			
Cotton	50					12	2	2			10												38		8				5			1	1		11
Rubber							39	9																3	12				1						8
Wheat	16	1	3	6	3	6		8	5	3	30	5							2	3	2				3	1	10		1	1					5
Wool	12	3		25	6	1		1	1	1	6	1									1								1	1					16

*Production less than 1 per cent of world total.
**Data not obtainable, but estimated production is included in figure for world total.
[1]Data for 1936; statistics for later years incomplete.
[2]Approximate production, estimated.
[3]From Southern Rhodesia.
[4]From Northern Rhodesia.

NOTE: Statistics of world production since 1929 are somewhat inadequate. Immediately after that year production was subnormal. More recently, military operations in Spain and China and the secretiveness of authoritarian governments have made it difficult to obtain complete data. The figures in the accompanying table therefore are approximations rather than accurate measurements, but they will suffice to indicate the general geographic distribution of essential war materials. In studying these statistics account should also be taken of the possible use of substitutes. In 1937, for example, Germany was reported to have produced nearly a million metric tons of gasoline from coal, as well as nearly 60,000 tons of reclaimed wool and 25,000 tons of synthetic or reclaimed rubber. The amount of world production of these reclaimed or synthetic products is not known and they are not included in the statistics here given. (Sources: *Minerals Yearbook, 1938*, compiled by the U. S. Bureau of Mines, and *Statistical Yearbook, 1938-39*, compiled by the League of Nations.)

PRESIDENT ROOSEVELT'S MESSAGE TO CONGRESS OF SEPTEMBER 21, 1939.[1]

I have asked the Congress to reassemble in extraordinary session in order that it may consider and act on the amendment of certain legislation, which, in my best judgment, so alters the historic foreign policy of the United States that it impairs the peaceful relations of the United States with foreign nations.

At the outset I proceed on the assumption that every member of the Senate and of the House of Representatives, and every member of the executive branch of the Government, including the President and his associates, personally and officially, are equally and without reservation in favor of such measures as will protect the neutrality, the safety and the integrity of our country and at the same time keep us out of war.

Because I am wholly willing to ascribe an honorable desire for peace to those who hold different views from my own as to what those measures should be, I trust that these gentlemen will be sufficiently generous to ascribe equally lofty purposes to those with whom they disagree.

Let no man or group in any walk of life assume exclusive protectorate over the future well-being of America—because I conceive that regardless of party or section the mantle of peace and of patriotism is wide enough to cover us all.

Let no group assume the exclusive label of the peace "bloc." We all belong to it.

I have at all times kept the Congress and the American people informed of events and trends in foreign affairs. I now review them in a spirit of understatement.

Since 1931 the use of force instead of the council table has constantly increased in the settlement of disputes between

[1]*New York Times,* September 22, 1939.

nations—except in the Western Hemisphere, where there has been only one war, now happily terminated.

During these years also the building up of vast armies, navies and storehouses of war has proceeded abroad with growing speed and intensity. But, during these years, and extending back even to the days of the Kellogg-Briand pact, the United States has constantly, consistently and conscientiously done all in its power to encourage peaceful settlements, to bring about reduction of armaments and to avert threatened wars. We have done this not only because any war anywhere necessarily hurts American security and American prosperity, but because of the more important fact that any war anywhere retards the progress of morality and religion and impairs the security of civilization itself.

For many years the primary purpose of our foreign policy has been that this nation and this Government should strive to the utmost to aid in avoiding war among other nations. But if and when war unhappily comes, the Government and the nation must exert every possible effort to avoid being drawn into the war.

The executive branch of the Government did its utmost, within our traditional policy of non-involvement, to aid in averting the present appalling war. Having thus striven and failed, this Government must lose no time or effort to keep the nation from being drawn into the war.

In my candid judgment we shall succeed in these efforts.

We are proud of the historical record of the United States and of all the Americas during all these years because we have thrown every ounce of our influence for peace into the scale of peace.

I note in passing what you will all remember—the long debates on the subject of what constitutes aggression, on the methods of determining who the aggressor might be, and on who the aggressor in past wars had been. Academically this may have been instructive as it may have been of interest to historians to discuss the pros and cons and the rights and wrongs of the world war during the decade that followed it.

But in the light of problems of today and tomorrow, responsibility for acts of aggression is not concealed, and the writing of the record can safely be left to future historians.

There has been sufficient realism in the United States to see how close to our own shores came dangerous paths which were being followed on other continents.

Last January I told the Congress that "a war which threatened to envelop the world in flames has been averted, but it has become increasingly clear that peace is not assured." By April new tensions had developed; a new crisis was in the making. Several nations with whom we had friendly diplomatic and commercial relations had lost, or were in the process of losing, their independent identity and sovereignty.

During the spring and summer the trend was definitely toward further acts of military conquest and away from peace. As late as the end of July I spoke to members of the Congress about the definite possibility of war. I should have called it the probability of war.

Last January, also, I spoke to this Congress of the need for further warning of new threats of conquest, military and economic; of challenge to religion, to democracy and to international good faith. I said:

"An ordering of society which relegates religion, democracy and good faith among nations to the background can find no place within it for the ideals of the Prince of Peace. The United States rejects such an ordering and retains its ancient faith."

"We know what might happen to us of the United States if the new philosophies of force were to encompass the other continents and invade our own. We, no more than other nations, can afford to be surrounded by the enemies of our faith and our humanity. Fortunate it is, therefore, that in this Western Hemisphere we have, under a common ideal of democratic government, a rich diversity of resources and of peoples functioning together in mutual respect and peace."

Last January, in the same message, I also said: "We have learned that when we deliberately try to legislate neutrality, our neutrality laws may operate unevenly and un-fairly—may actually give aid to an aggressor and deny it to the victim. The instinct of self-preservation should warn us that we ought not to let that happen any more."

It was because of what I foresaw last January from watching the trend of foreign affairs and their probable effect upon us that I recommended to the Congress in July of this year that changes be enacted in our neutrality law.

The essentials for American peace in the world have not changed since January. That is why I ask you again to re-examine our own legislation.

Beginning with the foundation of our constitutional gov-ernment in the year 1789, the American policy in respect to belligerent nations, with one notable exception, has been based on international law. Be it remembered that what we call international law has had as its primary objectives the avoid-ance of causes of war and the prevention of the extension of war.

The single exception was the policy adopted by this nation during the Napoleonic wars, when, seeking to avoid involve-ment, we acted for some years under the so-called Embargo and Non-Intercourse Acts. That policy turned out to be a disastrous failure—first, because it brought our own nation close to ruin, and, second, because it was the major cause of bringing us into active participation in European wars in our own War of 1812. It is merely reciting history to recall to you that one of the results of the policy of embargo and non-intercourse was the burning in 1814 of part of this Capitol in which we are assembled.

Our next deviation by statute from the sound principles of neutrality and peace through international law did not come for one hundred and thirty years. It was the so-called Neutrality Act of 1935—only four years ago—an act con-tinued in force by the joint resolution of May 1, 1937, despite grave doubts expressed as to its wisdom by many Senators and Representatives and by officials charged with the con-duct of our foreign relations, including myself. I regret that the Congress passed that act. I regret equally that I signed that act.

On July fourteenth of this year, I asked the Congress in the cause of peace and in the interest of real American neutrality and security to take action to change that act.

I now ask again that such action be taken in respect to that part of the act which is wholly inconsistent with ancient precepts of the law of nations—the embargo provisions. I ask it because they are, in my opinion, most vitally dangerous to American neutrality, American security and American peace.

These embargo provisions, as they exist today, prevent the sale to a belligerent by an American factory of any completed implements of war, but they allow the sale of many types of uncompleted implements of war, as well as all kinds of general material and supplies. They, furthermore, allow such products of industry and agriculture to be taken in American-flag ships to belligerent nations. There in itself— under the present law—lies definite danger to our neutrality and our peace.

From a purely material point of view, what is the advantage to us in sending all manner of articles across the ocean for final processing there, when we could give employment to thousands by doing it here? Incidentally, and again from the material point of view, by such employment we automatically aid our own national defense. And if abnormal profits appear in our midst even in time of peace, as a result of this increase of industry, I feel certain that the subject will be adequately dealt with at the coming regular session of the Congress.

Let me set forth the present paradox of the existing legislation in its simplest terms: If, prior to 1935, a general war had broken out in Europe, the United States would have sold to and bought from belligerent nations such goods and products of all kinds as the belligerent nations, with their existing facilities and geographical situations, were able to buy from us or sell to us.

This would have been the normal practice under the age-old doctrines of international law. Our prior position accepted the facts of geography and of conditions of land power and sea power alike as they existed in all parts of the world. If a war in Europe had broken out prior to 1935, there would have been no difference, for example, between our exports of sheets of aluminum and airplane wings; today there is an artificial legal difference.

Before 1935 there would have been no difference between the export of cotton and the export of gun cotton. Today there is. Before 1935 there would have been no difference between the shipment of brass tubing in pipe form and brass tubing in shell form. Today there is. Before 1935 there would have been no difference between the export of a motor truck and an armored motor truck. Today there is.

Let us be factual and recognize that a belligerent nation often needs wheat and lard and cotton for the survival of its population just as much as it needs anti-aircraft guns and anti-submarine depth-charges. Let those who seek to retain the present embargo position be wholly consistent and seek new legislation to cut off cloth and copper and meat and wheat and a thousand other articles from all of the nations at war.

I seek a greater consistency through the repeal of the embargo provisions, and a return to international law. I seek re-enactment of the historic and traditional American policy which, except for the disastrous interlude of the Embargo and Non-Intercourse Acts, has served us well for nearly a century and a half.

It has been erroneously said that return to that policy might bring us nearer to war. I give to you my deep and unalterable conviction, based on years of experience as a worker in the field of international peace, that by the repeal of the embargo the United States will more probably remain at peace than if the law remains as it stands today. I say this because with the repeal of the embargo this Government clearly and definitely will insist that American citizens and

American ships keep away from the immediate perils of the actual zones of conflict.

Repeal of the embargo and a return to international law are the crux of this issue.

The enactment of the embargo provisions did more than merely reverse our traditional policy. It had the effect of putting land powers on the same footing as naval powers, so far as sea-borne commerce was concerned. A land power which threatened war could thus feel assured in advance that any prospective sea-power antagonist would be weakened through denial of its ancient right to buy anything anywhere.

This, four years ago, gave a definite advantage to one belligerent as against another, not through his own strength or geographic position, but through an affirmative act of ours. Removal of the embargo is merely reverting to the sounder international practice, and pursuing in time of war as in time of peace our ordinary trade policies. This will be liked by some and disliked by others, depending on the view they take of the present war, but that is not the issue. The step I recommend is to put this country back on the solid footing of real and traditional neutrality.

When and if repeal of the embargo is accomplished, certain other phases of policy re-enforcing American safety should be considered. While nearly all of us are in agreement on their objectives, the only question relates to method.

I believe that American merchant vessels should, so far as possible, be restricted from entering danger zones. War zones may change so swiftly and so frequently in the days to come that it is impossible to fix them permanently by act of Congress; specific legislation may prevent adjustment to constant and quick change.

It seems, therefore, more practical to delimit them through action of the State Department and administrative agencies. The objective of restricting American ships from entering such zones may be attained by prohibiting such entry by the Congress; or the result can be substantially achieved by executive proclamation that all such voyages are solely at the risk of the American owners themselves.

The second objective is to prevent American citizens from traveling on belligerent vessels, or in danger areas. This can also be accomplished either by legislation, through continuance in force of certain provisions of existing law, or by proclamation making it clear to all Americans that any such travel is at their own risk.

The third objective, requiring the foreign buyer to take transfer of title in this country to commodities purchased by belligerents, is also a result which can be attained by legislation or substantially achieved through due notice by proclamation.

The fourth objective is the preventing of war credits to belligerents. This can be accomplished by maintaining in force existing provisions of law, or by proclamation making it clear that if credits are granted by American citizens to belligerents our Government will take no steps in the future to relieve them of risk or loss. The result of these last two will be to require all purchases to be made in cash and cargoes to be carried in the purchasers' own ships, at the purchasers' own risk.

Two other objectives have been amply attained by existing law, namely, regulating collection of funds in this country for belligerents, and the maintenance of a license system covering import and export of arms, ammunition and implements of war. Under present enactments, such arms cannot be carried to belligerent countries on American vessels, and this provision should not be disturbed.

The Congress, of course, should make its own choice of the method by which these safeguards are to be attained, so long as the method chosen will meet the needs of new and changing day to day situations and dangers.

To those who say that this program would involve a step toward war on our part, I reply that it offers far greater safeguards than we now possess or have ever possessed to protect American lives and property from danger. It is a positive program for giving safety. This means less likelihood of incidents and controversies which tend to draw us into conflict, as they did in the last World War. There lies the road to peace!

The position of the executive branch of the Government is that the age-old and time-honored doctrine of international law, coupled with these positive safeguards, is better calculated than any other means to keep us out of this war.

In respect to our own defense, you are aware that I have issued a proclamation setting forth "a national emergency in connection with the observance, safeguarding, and enforcement of neutrality and the strengthening of the national defense within the limits of peace-time authorizations." This was done solely to make wholly constitutional and legal certain obviously necessary measures.

I have authorized increases in the personnel of the army, navy, Marine Corps and Coast Guard, which will bring all four to a total still below peace-time strength as authorized by the Congress.

I have authorized the State Department to use, for the repatriation of Americans caught in the war zone, $500,000 already authorized by the Congress.

I have authorized the addition of 150 persons to the Department of Justice to be used in the protection of the United States against subversive foreign activities within our borders.

At this time I ask for no other authority from the Congress. At this time I see no need for further executive action under the proclamation of limited national emergency.

Therefore, I see no valid reason for the consideration of other legislation at this extraordinary session of the Congress.

It is, of course, possible that in the months to come unforeseen needs for further legislation may develop, but they are not imperative today.

These perilous days demand cooperation between us without trace of partisanship. Our acts must be guided by one single hard-headed thought—keeping America out of this war. In that spirit, I am asking the leaders of the two major parties in the Senate and in the House of Representatives to remain in Washington between the close of this extraordinary session and the beginning of the regular session on January third.

They have assured me that they will do so, and I expect to consult with them at frequent intervals on the course of events in foreign affairs and on the need for future action in this field, whether it be executive or legislative action.

Further, in the event of any future danger to the security of the United States or in the event of need for any new legislation of importance, I will immediately reconvene the Congress in another extraordinary session.

I should like to be able to offer the hope that the shadow over the world might swiftly pass. I can not. The facts compel my stating, with candor, that darker periods may lie ahead. The disaster is not of our making; no act of ours engendered the forces which assault the foundations of civilization. Yet we find ourselves affected to the core; our currents of commerce are changing, our minds are filled with new problems, our position in world affairs has already been altered.

In such circumstances our policy must be to appreciate in the deepest sense the true American interest. Rightly considered, this interest is not selfish. Destiny first made us, with our sister nations on this hemisphere, joint heirs of European culture. Fate seems now to compel us to assume the task of helping to maintain in the Western World a citadel wherein that civilization may be kept alive.

The peace, the integrity and the safety of the Americas— these must be kept firm and serene. In a period when it is sometimes said that free discussion is no longer compatible with national safety, may you by your deeds show the world that we of the United States are one people, of one mind, one spirit, one clear resolution, walking before God in the light of the living.

CHRONOLOGY OF EVENTS AFFECTING UNITED STATES NEUTRALITY LEGISLATION, 1933 TO DATE .

1933:

January:

10. In a message to Congress President Hoover urges ratification by the Senate of the Geneva Convention of 1925 for the supervision of international trade in arms and munitions of war, or if this is not possible, the adoption of legislation authorizing the President in his discretion to coöperate with other arms-manufacturing nations in prohibiting the shipment of arms for military purposes.

19. The Senate passes a joint resolution prohibiting the exportation, under certain conditions, of arms or munitions of war from the United States to any country or countries. (The House took no action at this session.)

April:

17. By a vote of 253 to 109 the House of Representatives, chosen at the same time Roosevelt was elected, approves the arms embargo resolution adopted by the Senate at the previous session and thus authorizes an embargo against an aggressor nation.

May:

27. The Senate Foreign Relations Committee amends the House resolution with a proviso that the embargo "shall apply impartially to all of the parties in a dispute." (There was no further action on the measure at this session of Congress.)

1934:

April:

19. The Senate appoints a special committee to investigate the traffic in arms and munitions of war.

249

May:

18. President Roosevelt sends a message to Congress in which he suggests international action for the supervision and control of the traffic in arms.

23. The House passes a joint resolution empowering the President to prohibit the sale of arms and munitions of war to Bolivia and Paraguay. The Senate passes a similar resolution on the 24th.

28. President Roosevelt signs the resolution authorizing an embargo on shipments of arms and munitions to Bolivia and Paraguay and by proclamation puts the ban into effect.

June:

29. President Roosevelt declares an embargo on the export of military material to Cuba, then under martial law, except when shipments are licensed by the Department of State.

September:

4. The special Senate committee appointed to investigate the activities of the munitions industry begins hearings in Washington.

December:

5. A border fray at Walwal, East Africa, in territory claimed by Ethiopia and Italy, results in casualties on both sides and foreshadows the Italo-Ethiopian war.

1935:

June:

6. The Senate consents to the ratification, with reservations, of the Geneva Convention of 1925 for the supervision of international trade in arms and munitions of war.

August:

7. The Export-Import Bank of Washington announces a policy of withholding credits to cover commodities which "look like munitions," and asks all exporters seeking credits for shipments of cotton to Italy, whether this material is to be used for munitions.

17. Representative McReynolds, Chairman of the House Committee on Foreign Affairs, offers a joint resolution empowering the President at his discretion to place an embargo on one or all of belligerents in the event of war and take other action for the promotion of peace.

20. Members of the Senate Munitions Investigating Committee threaten to conduct a filibuster against important domestic legislation unless prompt consideration is given to a neutrality measure.

21. The Senate Foreign Relations Committee reports a joint resolution providing a mandatory embargo on shipments of war materials to all belligerents in the event of a foreign war. The resolution is adopted after a brief discussion.

23. After being amended the Senate resolution is accepted by the House without a roll-call. The Senate concurs in the House amendment on the 24th.

31. President Roosevelt approves the neutrality resolution. The measure provides for a mandatory embargo on the shipment of arms and munitions and implements of war, but stipulates that it shall continue only until February 29, 1936. In signing it, the President criticizes the mandatory features and states that further study of the whole problem is desirable.

September:

19. The National Munitions Control Board, created under the neutrality resolution for the regulation of the traffic in war materials, holds its first meeting in Washington.

24. President Roosevelt proclaims list of war implements, the makers, importers and exporters of which must register with the Department of State before November 29.

October:

3. General Emilio de Bono, Italian Commander in Chief in Africa, announces the beginning of hostilities between Italy and Ethiopia.

5. President Roosevelt issues two proclamations, one declaring an arms embargo against Italy and Ethiopia, and the other admonishing American citizens that if they travel in vessels of either belligerent, they will do so at their own risk.

November:

2. League Coördinating Committee sets November 18 as the date on which the application of sanctions against Italy will become effective.

14. President Roosevelt orders the revocation of the embargo on shipment of arms and munitions to Bolivia and Paraguay. The Chaco war officially ended on the 29th.

1936:

January:

3. A new neutrality bill, sponsored by the Administration and designed to fix a permanent policy, is introduced in the House by Representative McReynolds and in the Senate by Senator Pittman.

February:

12. In lieu of new legislation, the Senate Foreign Relations Committee proposes to extend the existing law for fourteen months.

17. The House votes to extend the Neutrality Act to May 1, 1937, and the Senate concurs on the 18th. Amendments are added, however, including a ban on the granting of loans and credits to belligerents and exempting American republics, under certain conditions, from the operation of the law.

29. President Roosevelt approves the resolution extending the Neutrality Act.

May:

2. All organized resistance against Italy collapses when Emperor Haile Selassie flees from Ethiopia. The end of the Italo-Ethiopian war is announced by Premier Mussolini on the 5th when Italian troops occupy Addis Ababa.

June:

20. Following the end of the Italo-Ethiopian conflict President Roosevelt removes the embargo on the export of arms, munitions and implements of war to Italy and Ethiopia, in force since October 5, 1935, and withdraws the warning to American citizens not to travel on the vessels of either belligerent.

30. League Assembly meets in special session to consider the removal of sanctions against Italy. Report from the Bureau recommending the lifting of sanctions against Italy is adopted on July 4, and becomes effective on July 15. Great Britain and Soviet Russia end sanctions against Italy on July 10; other countries soon follow.

July:

17. A military revolt against the government of the Spanish Republic breaks out.

August:

21. Department of State announces, in reply to inquiries from munitions manufacturers, that sales to either faction in the Spanish civil war would be incompatible with the neutrality policy of the United States.

September:

9. The International Committee on Non-Intervention in Spain meets for the first time.

December:

28. In spite of its announced policy, the Department of State finds it necessary under the law to issue licenses for the shipment of planes, engines, etc., to the Loyalist government in Spain, since the Neutrality Act makes no provision for embargoes in case of civil war.

1937:

January:

6. Congress passes a joint resolution forbidding arms shipments to Spain. President Roosevelt signs the measure on the 8th.

10. Department of State issues warning that any American wishing to join either side in the Spanish civil war will do so without the protection of an American passport.

March:

3. The Senate adopts, by a vote of 63 to 6, a neutrality resolution introduced by Senator Pittman and designed to extend and replace existing legislation due to expire on May 1.

18. The House adopts, by a vote of 376 to 12, a neutrality resolution introduced by Representative McReynolds and designed to the same end.

April:

29. The Senate and the House agree on a compromise neutrality measure, which is signed by President Roosevelt on May 1. The most important new feature is the "cash-and-carry" provision.

July:

7. A clash between Chinese and Japanese soldiers near Peiping precipitates a new conflict between China and Japan.

September:

14. President Roosevelt states that merchant vessels owned by the United States Government will not carry arms or munitions to China or Japan, while privately owned vessels will do so at own risk.

26. Japanese troops occupy Shanghai after two months of fighting.

October:

5. In a speech at Chicago President Roosevelt advocates "quarantining" aggressor nations.

December:

7. Japanese troops occupy Nanking, China's capital.

12. Japanese airplanes bomb and sink the United States gunboat *Panay* and three Standard Oil vessels in the Yangtze River above Nanking, outside the war zone.

13. Representative Ludlow of Indiana obtains sufficient signatures for a vote in the House on the discharge of the Judiciary Committee from further consideration of his resolution providing for a constitutional amendment requiring approval by voters in a nation-wide referendum before Congress can declare war, except in case of actual invasion.

1938:

January:

10. The House, by a vote of 209 to 188, refuses to take the Ludlow war referendum resolution out of committee for consideration on the floor of the House.

March:

12. German troops enter Austria. The union with Germany is proclaimed from Vienna on the 13th.

June:

11. Secretary Hull, with reference to the Far Eastern conflict, reveals that American manufacturers have been urged to suspend the sale of American airplanes to countries bombing civilians and open cities.

16. United States adopts the Pittman resolution condemning "the inhuman bombing of civilian populations."

September:

29. Chancellor Hitler, Premier Mussolini, Prime Minister Chamberlain and Premier Daladier meet at Munich to settle the German-Czech dispute over the Sudeten area. Most of Chancellor Hitler's demands outlined in the Godesberg memorandum are met. The Czech Government protests against the decision, but accepts it on the 30th, declaring that its people can do nothing except yield to a decision taken "without them and against them."

October:

21-25. With the occupation of Canton on the 22nd and Hankow on the 25th, control is established by Japan over much of China; but the war still goes on.

1939:

January:

4. In his message to Congress President Roosevelt states that aggressor nations may be notified of American public opinion by "many measures short of war, but stronger and more effective than mere words."

26. Insurgent General Franco's troops occupy Barcelona.

March:

14. Following difficulties between the Czechs and Slovaks, Chancellor Hitler intervenes and German troops invade Czechoslovakia.

15. Chancellor Hitler enters Prague. A decree proclaiming the Czech provinces of Bohemia and Moravia a protectorate of the Reich is broadcast by the German Foreign Minister on the 16th. Slovakia is taken under German protection at her own request. Incorporation of the Carpatho-Ukraine in Hungary is announced in Budapest on the 16th.

28. With the surrender of Madrid without further resistance and the flight of Spanish Loyalist officials from the country, the Spanish civil war comes to a close.

March:

20. Senator Pittman introduces a neutrality resolution to be known as the "Peace Act of 1939" and permitting the export of arms and munitions to all belligerents in time of war on a "cash-and-carry" basis.

April:

5. Henry L. Stimson, former Secretary of State, is the first witness to appear at the hearings of the Senate Foreign Relations Committee on the proposed revision of the Neutrality Act. He urges that the President be given wider discretion to defend "the vital interests of the United States" by throwing its moral and material resources against aggressor nations.

6. Bernard M. Baruch, former chairman of the War Industries Board, at neutrality hearings before the Senate Foreign Relations Committee, declares that the best way for the United States to keep out of war is to make its goods and supplies available to all belligerents without discrimination, as provided in the "cash-and-carry" plan.

22. As one "measure short of war" the United States applies an increase of 25 per cent. in countervailing duties on all dutiable German goods, unless it is shown that German exports are not subsidized.

May:

1. The "cash and carry" provision of the Neutrality Act expires.

27. In letters to the chairmen of the Senate Foreign Relations Committee and the House Committee on Foreign Affairs, Secretary Hull submits proposals for the revision of the Neutrality Act, which include elimination of the arms embargo provision in the existing legislation.

29. Representative Bloom of New York introduces a neutrality resolution based on Secretary Hull's proposals.

June:

13. The House Committee on Foreign Affairs recommends favorable action on the Bloom neutrality resolution.

30. The House amends and passes the Bloom resolution by a vote of 200 to 188. (See below, July 11.)

July:

5. As another "measure short of war," the United States increases countervailing duties on Italian silks.

11. The Senate Foreign Relations Committee, by a vote of 12 to 11, defers revision of the Neutrality Act until the next session of Congress.

14. President Roosevelt sends a special message to Congress urging enactment of neutrality legislation at the current session of Congress.

26. As another "measure short of war," the United States gives formal notice to Japan of abrogation of its commercial treaty of 1911 with that country.

September:

1. Invasion of Poland by German troops marks the beginning of the European war.

3. Great Britain and France declare war against Germany.

3. President Roosevelt delivers a radio address on the position of the United States.

3. Australia declares war against Germany.

4. New Zealand declares war against Germany.

4. Department of State restricts travel of American citizens in Europe.

5. The Union of South Africa breaks off diplomatic relations with Germany.

5. Following the outbreak of war in Europe, President Roosevelt issues two proclamations, one setting forth American neutrality under the terms of international law, and the other complying with the requirements of the Neutrality Act prohibiting the exportation of "arms, ammunition, and implements of war" to Germany, Poland, France, the United Kingdom, India, Australia and New Zealand.

5-6. Various regulations under the U. S. Neutrality Act are issued.

8. President Roosevelt extends the provisions of the Neutrality Act to the Union of South Africa after notification by that country that it had entered the war on Great Britain's side.

9. Canada declares war against Germany.

10. President Roosevelt extends the provisions of the Neutrality Act to Canada.

14. President Roosevelt summons Congress to meet on September 21 in special session. Secretary Hull issues statement reserving all American rights under international law.

21. United States Congress assembles in special session and hears President Roosevelt deliver a message on neutrality legislation.

BIBLIOGRAPHY ON AMERICAN NEUTRALITY

GENERAL, HISTORICAL AND LEGAL

Books:

ADAMS, HENRY. History of the United States: 1801 to 1817. New edition. New York, Scribner, 1921, 9v.

BEMIS, GEORGE. American Neutrality: Its Honorable Past, Its Expedient Future. Boston, Little, Brown, 1866, 211p.

BEMIS, SAMUEL FLAGG. Diplomacy of the American Revolution. New York, Appleton-Century, 1935, 293p. (Foundations of American Diplomacy, 1775-1823, V. I.)

—————. A Diplomatic History of the United States. New York, Holt, 1936, 881p.

BORCHARD, EDWIN, and LAGE, WILLIAM POTTER. Neutrality for the United States. New Haven, Yale University Press, 1937, 380p.

COHN, GEORG. Neo-Neutrality. New York, Columbia University Press, 1939, 388p.

CRECRAFT, EARL W. Freedom of the Seas. New York, Appleton-Century, 1935, 304p.

DEÁK, FRANCIS, ed. Treaty Provisions. Defining Neutral Rights and Duties, 1778-1936. Washington, Government Printing Office, 1937, 150p.

FENWICK, CHARLES G. Neutrality Laws of the United States. Washington, Carnegie Endowment, 1913, 200p.

HYDE, CHARLES C. International Law, Chiefly as Interpreted and Applied by the United States. Boston, Little, Brown, 1922, 2v.

HYNEMAN, CHARLES S. First American Neutrality. Urbana, University of Illinois, 1934, 178p.

JESSUP, PHILIP C., ed. Neutrality: Its History, Economics and Law. New York, Columbia University Press, 1935-1936, 4v. (V. I. "The Origins" by Philip C. Jessup and Francis Deák. V. II. "The Napoleonic Period" by W. A. Phillips and A. H. Reede. V. III. "The World War Period" by Edgar Turlington. V. IV. "Today and Tomorrow" by Philip C. Jessup.)

MAHAN, ALFRED THAYER. Sea Power in Its Relations to the War of 1812. Boston, Little, Brown, 1919, 2v.

MOORE, JOHN BASSETT. Digest of International Law. Washington, Government Printing Office, 1906, 8v.

————————. International Law and Some Current Illusions. New York, Macmillan, 1924, 381p.

————————. The Principles of American Diplomacy. New York, Harper, 1918.

Rights and Duties of Neutral States in Naval and Aerial War; Draft Convention, with Comment, Prepared by the Research in International Law of the Harvard Law School. (*American Journal of International Law,* Supplement, July, 1939, pp. 167-817.)

SAVAGE, CARLTON. Policy of the United States Toward Maritime Commerce in War. Washington, Government Printing Office, 1934-1936, 2v. (V. I. 1776-1914. V. II. 1914-1918, with documents.)

SCOTT, JAMES BROWN, ed. The Controversy over Neutral Rights between the United States and France, 1797-1800. New York, Oxford, 1917, 510p.

SEARS, LOUIS MARTIN. Jefferson and the Embargo. Durham, N. C., Duke University Press, 1927, 340p.

THOMAS, CHARLES M. American Neutrality in 1793. New York, Columbia University Press, 1931, 295p.

U. S. LAWS, STATUTES, ETC. The Laws of Neutrality as Existing on August 1, 1914. Washington, Government Printing Office, 1918, 578p.

WRIGHT, QUINCY. The Future of Neutrality. (In *International Conciliation*, September, 1928, No. 242.)

WRIGHT, QUINCY, ed. Neutrality and Collective Security, by Sir Alfred Zimmern . . . William Edward Dodd . . . Charles Warren . . . Edwin DeWitt Dickinson . . . Chicago, The University of Chicago Press, 1936, 276p. (Lectures on the Harris Foundation, 1936.)

WORLD WAR PERIOD

Books:

ARNETT, ALEX MATHEWS. Claude Kitchin and the Wilson War Policies. Boston, Little, Brown, 1937, 341p.

BAKER, NEWTON D. Why We Went to War. Published for the Council on Foreign Relations. New York, Harper, 1936, 199p.

BAKER, RAY STANNARD, and DODD, W. E., eds. Public Papers of Woodrow Wilson. New York, Harper, 1926, V. III-IV.

BAKER, RAY STANNARD. Woodrow Wilson, Life and Letters; V. V, Neutrality, 1914-1915; and V. VI, Facing War, 1915-1917. New York, Doubleday, 1935 and 1937.

GARNER, JAMES W. International Law and the World War. New York, Longmans, 1920, 2v.

GRATTAN, C. HARTLEY. Why We Fought. New York, Vanguard, 1929, 453p.

GREY, EDWARD GREY, 1st VISCOUNT. Twenty-five Years, 1892-1916. New York, Stokes, 1925, 2v.

HENDRICK, BURTON J. The Life and Letters of Walter H. Page. New York, Doubleday, 1922-1926, 3v. in 4 parts.

HOUSE, EDWARD M. Intimate Papers. Boston, Houghton, 1926-1928, 4v.

LANSING, ROBERT. War Memoirs. Indianapolis, Bobbs-Merrill, 1935, 383p.

MILLIS, WALTER. Road to War: America, 1914-1917. Boston, Houghton, 1935, 466p.

MORRISSEY, ALICE M. American Defense of Neutral Rights, 1914-1917. Cambridge, Harvard University Press, 1939, 230p.

Papers Relating to the Foreign Relations of the United States: The World War. Supplements to 1914, 1915, 1916 and 1917. Washington, Government Printing Office, 1928-1932.

PAXSON, FREDERIC L. American Democracy and the World War. V. I, Pre-War Years, 1913-1917. Boston, Houghton, 1936, 427p.

PETERSON, H. C. Propaganda for War: The Campaign against American Neutrality, 1914-1917. Norman, University of Oklahoma Press, 1939, 357p.

SEYMOUR, CHARLES. American Diplomacy during the World War. Baltimore, Johns Hopkins Press, 1934, 417p.

————. American Neutrality, 1914-1917. New Haven, Yale University Press, 1935, 187p.

TANSILL, CHARLES CALLAN. America Goes to War. Boston, Little, Brown, 1938, 731p.

U. S. DEPARTMENT OF STATE. Neutrality Proclamations, 1914-1918. Washington, Government Printing Office, 1919, 64p.

————. Diplomatic Correspondence with Belligerent Governments Relating to Neutral Rights and Commerce. Washington, Government Printing Office, 1915, 2v. (European War Nos. 1 and 2.)

————. Diplomatic Correspondence with Belligerent Governments Relating to Neutral Rights and Duties. Washington, Government Printing Office, 1916-1918, 2v. (European War Nos. 3 and 4.)

Periodicals:

BAILEY, THOMAS A. The Sinking of the Lusitania. (In *American Historical Review,* October, 1935, p. 54-73.)

BUCHANAN, RUSSELL. Theodore Roosevelt and American Neutrality, 1914-1917. (In *American Historical Review,* July, 1938, p. 775-790.)

PHILLIPS, ETHEL C. American Participation in Belligerent Commercial Controls 1914-1917. (In *American Journal of International Law,* October, 1933, p. 675-693.)

SEYMOUR, CHARLES. American Neutrality: Experience of 1914-1917. (In *Foreign Affairs,* October, 1935, p. 26-36.)

POST WAR PERIOD

Books:

AMERICAN SOCIETY OF INTERNATIONAL LAW. Proceedings of the 27th Annual Meeting, April 27-29, 1933. Washington, The Society, 1933. (Includes addresses on neutrality by Charles Warren and Philip C. Jessup.)

——————. Proceedings of the 29th Annual Meeting, April 25-27, 1935. Washington, The Society, 1935. (Including addresses by: E. D. Dickinson, J. Dickinson, J. L. King, F. K. Nielson, James Brown Scott, Henry L. Stimson and L. H. Woolsey.)

BEARD, CHARLES A. The Devil Theory of War; an Inquiry into the Nature of History and the Possibility of Keeping Out of War. New York, Vanguard, 1936, 124p.

BRADLEY, PHILLIPS. Can We Stay Out of War? New York, Norton, 1936, 288p.

BUELL, RAYMOND LESLIE. American Neutrality and Collective Security. Geneva, Geneva Research Center, 1935, 29p. (Geneva Special Studies, V. VI, No. 6, 1935.)

FLEMING, DENNA FRANK. The United States and World Organization, 1920-1933. New York, Columbia University Press, 1938, 569p.

INTERNATIONAL AMERICAN CONFERENCE, 6th, HAVANA, 1928. Maritime Neutrality. Convention between the United States of America and Other American Republics. Signed at Havana, February 20, 1928. Washington, Government Phinting Office, 1932, 9p. (Treaty Series, No. 845.)

JESSUP, PHILIP C. American Neutrality and International Police. Boston, 1928, 170p. (World Peace Foundation Pamphlets, V. XI, No. 3.)

PADELFORD, NORMAN J. International Law and Diplomacy in the Spanish Civil Strife. New York, Macmillan, 1939, 710p.

RAUSHENBUSH, STEPHEN and RAUSHENBUSH, JOAN. The Final Choice; America between Europe and Asia. New York, Reynal, 1937, 331p.

SHEPARDSON, WHITNEY H. and SCROGGS, W. O. United States in World Affairs, 1934-1938. New York, Council on Foreign Relations, 1935-1939. 4 v.

STALEY, EUGENE. War Losses to a Neutral; an Analysis of the Cost to the United States of Cash and Carry, Neutrality Embargoes, Economic Sanctions, and other Policies in the Far Eastern Conflict. New York, League of Nations Association, 1937, 78p.

UNITED STATES. CONGRESS. HOUSE. COMMITTEE ON FOREIGN AFFAIRS. American Neutrality Policy. Hearings ... June to July, 1935. Washington, Government Printing Office, 1935, 68p.

————. American Neutrality Policy. Hearings . . . January, 1936. Washington, Government Printing Office, 1936, 306p.

————. American Neutrality Policy. Hearings . . . February, 1937. Washington, Government Printing Office, 1937, 177p.

————. American Neutrality Policy. Hearings . . . April to May, 1939. Washington, Government Printing Office, 1939, 639p.

————. American Neutrality Policy. Editorials Submitted to the Committee . . . Relative to H. J. Res. 306, The Neutrality Act of 1939. Revised Edition. Washington, Government Printing Office, 1939, 62p.

UNITED STATES. CONGRESS. SENATE. COMMITTEE ON FOREIGN RELATIONS. Neutrality. Hearings . . . January to February, 1936. Washington, Government Printing Office, 1936, 302p.

————. Neutrality. Hearings . . . February, 1937. Washington, Government Printing Office, 1937, 25p.

————. Neutrality, Peace Legislation, and Our Foreign Policy. Hearings . . . April to May, 1939. Washington, Government Printing Office, 1939, 613p.

UNITED STATES. DEPARTMENT OF STATE. International Traffic in Arms; Laws and Regulations Administered by the Secretary of State Governing the International Traffic in Arms, Ammunition, and Implements of War. 1st-5th Editions. Washington, Government Printing Office, 1935-1938.

UNITED STATES PRESIDENT, 1929-1933 (HOOVER). Address of President Hoover at the Ceremonies on the Eleventh Anniversary of Armistice Day . . . November 11, 1929. Washington, Government Printing Office, 1929, 7p.

UNITED STATES PRESIDENT, 1933-   (FRANKLIN D. ROOSEVELT). Elimination of Weapons of Offensive Warfare. Message from the President of the United States . . . to the Sovereigns and Presidents of Those Nations Participating in the Disarmament Conferences and the World Monetary and Economic Conference. Washington, Government Printing Office, 1933, 6p. (73d Congress, 1st Session. House Document 36.)

Periodicals:

BARUCH, BERNARD. Cash and Carry. (In *Today,* November 2, 1935, p. 6-7.)

——————. Neutrality. (In *Current History,* June, 1936, p. 32-44.)

BOYE, THORVALD. Shall a State Which Goes to War in Violation of the Kellogg-Briand Pact Have a Belligerent's Rights in Respect of Neutrals? (In *American Journal of International Law,* October, 1930, p. 766-770.)

BRADLEY, PHILLIPS. Neutrality—as of 1936 and 1937. (In *American Political Science Review,* February, 1937, p. 100-113.)

CHAMBERLAIN, JOSEPH P. The Embargo Resolutions and Neutrality. New York, Carnegie Endowment for International Peace, 90 p. (In *International Conciliation,* June, 1929, No. 251.)

CLARK, BENNETT CHAMP. Detour Around War. (In *Harpers,* December, 1935, p. 1-9.)

COUDERT, FREDERIC R. Can Present Legislation Guarantee Future Neutrality? (In *International Conciliation,* February, 1937, No. 327.)

DAVIS, NORMAN H. World Stability and the Sanctity of Treaties. Address before *New York Herald Tribune* Forum on Current Problems, October 15, 1935. (In *New York Herald Tribune,* October 16, 1935, p. 15.)

DEÁK, FRANCIS. The Pitfalls of the New American Neutrality. (In *International Conciliation,* May, 1938, No. 340.) Contains also: If War Comes, What Will America's Policy Be?, by George S. Montgomery, Jr.

DULLES, ALLEN W. The Cost of Peace. (In *Foreign Affairs,* July, 1934, p. 567-578.)

DULLES, ALLEN W. and ARMSTRONG, HAMILTON FISH. Legislating Peace. (In *Foreign Affairs,* October, 1938, p. 1-12.)

EAGLETON, CLYDE. Neutrality and the Capper Resolution. (In *New York University Law Review,* May, 1929, p. 346-364.)

—————. Revision of the Neutrality Act. (In *American Journal of International Law,* January, 1939, p. 119-126.)

FENWICK, CHARLES G. Neutrality and International Organization. (In *American Journal of International Law,* April, 1934, p. 334-339.)

FINCH, GEORGE A. The United States and the Spanish Civil War. (In *American Journal of International Law,* January, 1937, p. 74-81.)

FOREIGN POLICY REPORTS. New York, Foreign Policy Association.

>V. IV, No. 1. Neutral Rights and Maritime Law. 1928, 18p.

>V. IV, No. 2. American Neutrality and League Wars. 1928, 16p.

>V. XI, No. 3. American Neutrality in a Future War. 1935, 12p.

>V. XI, No. 23. The New American Neutrality. 1936, 16p.

>V. XIII, No. 14. The Neutrality Act of 1937. 1937, 16p.

>V. XIII, No. 17. U. S. Neutrality in the Spanish Conflict. 1937, 12p.

>V. XV, No. 3. Economic Problems of United States Neutrality in Wartime. 1939, 12p.

GARNER, JAMES W. The United States Neutrality Act of 1937. (In *American Journal of International Law,* July, 1937, p. 385-397.)

GREY, EDWARD GREY, 1ST VISCOUNT. Freedom of the Seas. (In *Foreign Affairs,* April, 1930, p. 325-335.)

HYDE, CHARLES CHENEY. The United States as a Neutral. (In *Yale Law Journal,* February, 1936, p. 608-621.)

INTERNATIONAL COMMISSION OF JURISTS. Public International Law, Projects to be Submitted for the Consideration of the Sixth International Conference of American States. (In *American Journal of International Law,* January, 1928, Supplement, p. 234-239.)

JESSUP, PHILIP C. Neutrality Legislation—1937. (In *American Journal of International Law,* April, 1937, p. 306-313.)

——————. Toward further neutrality legislation. (In *American Journal of International Law,* April, 1936, p. 262-265.)

——————. The Spanish Rebellion and International Law. (In *Foreign Affairs,* January, 1937, p. 260-279.)

MOORE, JOHN BASSETT. Appeal to Reason. (In *Foreign Affairs,* July, 1933, p. 547-588.)

NATIONAL PEACE CONFERENCE. Tentative Redraft of the Neutrality Act of August 31, 1935. Prepared by a Committee, James T. Shotwell, Chairman. (In *New York Times,* December 26, 1935, p. 10-11.)

NATIONAL PEACE CONFERENCE. A study of Neutrality Legislation; Report of a Committee of the National Peace Conference, with an introduction by James T. Shotwell. (In *International Conciliation,* January, 1936, No. 316.)

PATTERSON, ERNEST MINOR, ed. The Attainment and maintenance of World Peace . . . Supplement: Economic Aspects of Neutrality . . . (In *Annals of the American Academy of Political and Social Science,* July, 1936, p. 1-251.) Contains articles on U. S. Neutrality by Allen W. Dulles, Felix Morley, Ernest Minor Patterson, and Elbert D. Thomas.

——————. The United States and World War. (In *Annals of the American Academy of Political and Social Science,* July 1937, p. 1-155.) Contains articles on U. S. Neutrality by Charles G. Fenwick, George Soule, Philip C. Jessup, and William R. Castle, Jr.

SCOTT, JAMES BROWN. Neutrality of the United States. (In *American Journal of International Law,* October, 1935, p. 644-652.)

STIMSON, HENRY L. The Dangers of Neutrality: Letter to the Editor. (In *New York Times,* October 11, 1935.)

——————. Neutrality and War Prevention. (In *Proceedings of the American Society of International Law,* 1935, p. 121-129.) Reprinted in *International Conciliation,* September, 1935, No. 312.

——————. The Pact of Paris: Three Years of Development. (In *Foreign Affairs,* October, 1932, Special Supplement.)

——————. The Sale of Arms and Munitions to the Spanish Loyalist Government: Letter to the Editor. (In *New York Times,* January 24, 1939.) Reply by Martin Conboy: Letter to the Editor. (In *New York Times,* January 26, 1939.) Rebuttal by Charles C. Burlingham and Philip C. Jessup: Letter to the Editor. (In *New York Times,* January 31, 1939.)

WARREN, CHARLES. Belligerent Aircraft, Neutral Trade and Unpreparedness. (In *American Journal of International Law,* April, 1935, p. 197-205.)

——————. Contraband and Neutral Trade. (In *Proceedings of The Academy of Political Science,* 1934, p. 185-194.)

——————. Prepare for Neutrality. (In *Yale Review,* March, 1935, p. 467-478.)

——————. Safeguards to Neutrality. (In *Foreign Affairs,* January, 1936, p. 199-215.)

——————. Troubles of a Neutral. (In *Foreign Affairs,* April, 1934, p. 377-394.)

4427

Date Due

MAY 20			
MAY 16 '56			
NOV 25 '69			